The School Survival Guide For Kids With LD*

*(Learning Differences)

By Rhoda Woods Cummings, Ed.D.
and
Gary L. Fisher, Ph.D.

Edited by Pamela Espeland

Free Spirit®
PUBLISHING

Library of Congress Cataloging-in-Publication Data
    Cummings, Rhoda Woods.
      The school survival guide for kids with LD* *learning differences / by
    Rhoda Woods Cummings and Gary L. Fisher.
        p.   cm.
      Includes bibliographical references (p.) and index.
      Summary: Discusses how children with "learning differences" can
    get along better in school.
      ISBN 0-915793-32-6
      1. Learning disabled children—Education—United States—
    Handbooks, manuals, etc.—Juvenile literature. 2. Learning
    disabilities—United States—Handbooks, manuals, etc.—Juvenile
    literature. [1. Learning disabilities.]
    I. Fisher, Gary L. II. Title.
    LC4705.C86 1991   91-14489
    371.9—dc20   CIP
                                                                   AC

10 9 8 7 6 5
Printed in the United States of America

Cover and book design by MacLean & Tuminelly
Illustrations by Jackie Urbanovic
Line illustrations by Lisa Wagner

Free Spirit Publishing Inc.
400 First Avenue North, Suite 616
Minneapolis, MN 55401
(612) 338-2068

"Practice 'IN' and 'AGO'" on page 47 and "Use your pointer finger to
subtract through 10" on page 93 are from *Teaching Mathematics to the
Learning Disabled* by Nancy S. Bley and Carol A. Thornton. Used with
permission of PRO-ED.

Dedication

To our children,
Carter and Courtney,
Colin and Aaron

Acknowledgments

Thanks to Sharon Maddux, a great teacher, for her insight and help with the math tricks.

Thanks to our publisher, Judy Galbraith, and our editor, Pamela Espeland. We give them a bunch of information, and they turn it into books that children read and respond to—we appreciate the work they do.

A special thanks to all the kids who read our first book and wrote to us with questions and ideas. Keep reading and writing—we get chills when we hear from you. This book is a direct result of your letters.

Meet the Authors

Hello! My name is Rhoda Cummings. I studied special education in college. Now I teach it to students at the University of Nevada in Reno. I used to teach English and Social Studies to seventh graders. I have a grown-up son named Carter who has LD. Carter lives in Reno, has his own apartment, drives his own car, and has a full-time job. I have written books for teachers and parents of kids with LD. This is the second book Gary and I have written for kids with LD.

Hi! I'm Gary Fisher. I went to college for many years to study LD, and I have written about LD. Most importantly, I have worked with over 1,000 kids with LD. Some of them know me as Dr. Fisher, their school psychologist. For the past several years, I have lived in Truckee, California, and I teach at the University of Nevada in Reno. I help school counselors and school psychologists learn to work with all kinds of children, including kids with LD.

Contents

Chapter 16:

Chapter 17:

Chapter 18:

Introduction

Maybe you have read our first book, *The Survival Guide For Kids With LD*. In that book, we wrote about what LD means. Some people say it means "learning disabled." Others say it means "learning different." When we say LD, we always mean "learning different." We believe that everyone learns in their own way.

In our first book, we also wrote about what LD *does not* mean. It *does not* mean you are retarded! It *does not* mean you are dumb! It *does not* mean you are lazy! It *does not* mean you will have a low-paying job when you grow up!

We also wrote about ways to get along at home. We gave tips for making and keeping friends. We shared ideas for dealing with sad, hurt, angry feelings. We even gave ten ways to get along better in school.

Why We Wrote This Book

Many kids who read our first book have written letters to us. They have told us how good it feels to know that they are not retarded or dumb. We are happy that our book helps kids with LD feel better about themselves.

Some kids who wrote to us asked us to write back. They wanted to know more about how to get along better in school. They wanted to know more about how to learn better. Some of these kids worry because they do not read as well as other students. Some are confused about math. Many have trouble with spelling. Some feel bad because their writing is messy.

Kids also wanted to know more about how to organize their time. They asked if computers could help them learn better. They wanted more tips for making and keeping friends. They wanted to know how to stay out of trouble at school.

We try to write back to everyone who sends us a letter, so we wrote a lot of letters to kids. We gave them ideas about how to get along better and learn better in school. Finally we thought, "Maybe we should put all of these ideas down in another book." That is why we wrote *The School Survival Guide For Kids With LD.*

How To Use This Book

You will see that this book has three main parts. Part One is called "Ways To Make School Easier And More Fun." Part Two is called "School Tools For Learning." Part Three is called "Ways To Keep School Cool."

Each part has chapters. Each chapter gives different ways to get along better and learn better in school. You may already know about some of these ways. You may already use them in school. If you want to, you can read about them and practice them some more. Or you can skip ahead to find other ways you do not already know about.

★ Learn how to get computer time on pages 27–29.

★ For tips on handling testing, see pages 40–42.

★ Learn how to ask adults for help on pages 54–55.

★ Find out about a word bank on pages 62–63 and 78.

★ Learn about dictionaries for people who cannot spell well on page 82.

★ Practice a great way to solve problems on pages 124–127.

★ Find out eight ways to rescue recess on pages 129–131.

★ If you get into serious trouble, see pages 138–139.

After you finish reading *The School Survival Guide*, you may want to write us a letter. We would be glad to hear from you. Let us know how our book helped you. Or give us some ideas for making it better. You can send your letter to:

Rhoda Cummings and Gary Fisher
c/o Free Spirit Publishing Inc.
400 First Avenue North, Suite 616
Minneapolis, MN 55401

Best Wishes,
Rhoda Cummings and Gary Fisher

PART ONE:

WAYS TO MAKE SCHOOL EASIER AND MORE FUN

Chapter 1

You Can Get Organized

Many kids with LD could learn better if they just got organized. School would be easier if they kept track of their materials. Learning would be easier if they remembered the things they are supposed to do. They would get better grades if they did their homework on time. Classes would be more fun if they brought the right materials.

If you need to get organized, try some of the ideas in this chapter.

Eight Ways To Manage Your Time

Jennifer* is a friend of ours with LD who gets low grades. One reason is because she turns in many late assignments.

We asked Jennifer why she had this problem. She said, "I am a slow reader. It takes me a long time to read my assignments. I don't have enough time left for my homework."

We asked Jennifer's teacher about the problem. Her teacher said, "I know that Jennifer is a slow reader. That's why I give Jennifer her assignments early. But she still turns her work in late."

---

* *"Jennifer" is not the real name of our friend. In this book, we do not use the real names of people we know. We use made-up names instead, to respect their privacy.*

Next, we talked to Jennifer's mother. Her mother said, "The teacher is right. Jennifer gets her assignments in plenty of time to finish them. But she always waits until the last minute to do them."

Slow reading is not Jennifer's real problem. Her real problem is waiting until the last minute to do her homework. This is called "procrastinating."

Procrastinate
prō KRAS tə NĀT

To procrastinate means "to put off doing something you should do right away." When you procrastinate, you leave things until the last minute. You do not give yourself enough time to do them right. Then you worry about doing them wrong. You may give up and not do them at all. Procrastination can become a bad habit.

Do you procrastinate? If you do, here are eight ways to manage your time better. Even if you do not procrastinate, you may want to try some of these ideas.

1. *Follow a daily routine.*

Routine
rōō TĒN

Maybe you get up every morning, eat breakfast, and get dressed. Or maybe you get dressed first, then eat breakfast. Your regular way of doing things is called your "routine." A routine makes it easier to remember things you are supposed to do.

You can make a daily routine for school. Ask someone to help you. This can be your classroom teacher, your LD teacher, a parent, or another adult. It can be a big brother or sister or friend.

On page 148, you will find a form called "My Routine." You can copy this form or make your own. Here is an example of a partly filled-in form.

MY ROUTINE					
TIME	MON	TUES	WED	THURS	FRI
7:00	Breakfast				
8:00	To school				
9:00	Reading				
10:00	Math				
11:00	Soc. Studi.				
12:00	Lunch				
1:00	Spelling				
2:00	Recess				
3:00	Science				

Once you make your routine, use it! Each day when you get up, look at your routine for that day. This will help you to remember what you are supposed to do.

If you want, you can have your routine laminated (covered with plastic). This will keep it from getting wrinkled or torn. Some public schools and libraries have laminating machines. Many copy shops have them, too. Plan to spend about $1.00 or $2.00.

2. Keep an assignment book.

When your teacher gives you an assignment, write it down in your assignment book. Count how many days are left before it is due. Then start working on the assignment right away.

LOOK-AT-THE-MONTH OF: _April_

1 ___
2 ___
3 ___
4 ___
5 _Social studies paper due in 15 days_
6 ___
7 ___
8 ___
9 ___
10 _Social studies paper due in 10 days_
11 ___
12 ___
13 ___
14 ___
15 ___
16 ___
17 ___
18 ___
19 ___
20 _Social studies paper due TODAY!!_
21 ___
22 ___
23 ___
24 ___
25 ___
26 ___
27 ___
28 ___
29 ___
30 ___
31 ___

3. Chart your time.

On page 149, you will find a "Time Chart" form. Make five copies of this form. Every school day for a week, write down how you spend your time. Here is an example of a filled-in form.

TIME CHART

Day: Monday

Activity	Time
★ Breakfast	30 minutes
★ Get dressed	30 minutes
★ School	7 hours
★ Homework	
★ Math	1 hour
★ Spelling	30 minutes
★ Reading	30 minutes
★ Dinner	1 hour

When the week is over, look at your time charts. Ask a helper to look at them with you. What can you learn from your time charts? Can you use them to plan ahead?

Make five new copies of the Time Chart form, one for each day of next week. Write down what you will do each day. Then write down how much time you think each activity will take. Work with your helper to do this.

Every time you finish an activity, draw a star next to it. Or buy colored stars to stick on your charts. See how many stars you can give yourself by the end of the week.

4. Learn to estimate times.

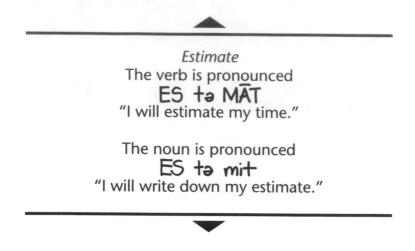

Estimate
The verb is pronounced
ES tə MĀT
"I will estimate my time."

The noun is pronounced
ES tə mit
"I will write down my estimate."

Sometimes students think an assignment will not take much time to do. They procrastinate and do not get it done on time.

When you get an assignment, try to think about how long it will take to get it done. What are all of the things you need to do? How long will it take to do each one? Try to get a rough idea of how much total time you will need. This is called "estimating."

Write down your estimate. Then show it to an adult. If the adult thinks your assignment will take longer, listen. Write down the adult's estimate of how much time it will take. Give yourself more time to do your assignment.

5. Make "Things-To-Do" lists.

Each day after school, make a list of things you need to do before bedtime. Think about how long it will take to do each one. When you finish each thing, check it off on your list.

On page 150, you will find a "Things To Do" list form you can use.

6. Do the hardest job first.

When you sit down to do your homework, do the hardest assignments first. This is the time when you will have the most energy and be the most awake. Save the easiest assignments for last.

7. Make a list of "time stealers."

What things keep you from doing your homework? Do you stop working to talk on the phone, watch TV, play a video game, get a snack, or daydream?

Make a list of these "time stealers." Tell yourself you can do them when your homework is finished.

8. Reward yourself.

When you follow your routine, or finish an assignment on time, reward yourself. Do something you enjoy. This might be something you wrote on your "time stealers" list.

Manage Your Materials

Michael is another friend of ours with LD. His teacher used to get mad at him because he never brought the right materials to class. "I brought my math book to reading," he says. "Or I brought my spelling list to math class."

Michael keeps his materials in a locker. He is usually in a big hurry to get his materials and get to class on time. He just grabs his books and notebooks without paying much attention.

We told Michael to color-code his materials. For reading, he used the color red. He covered his reading book in red paper and bought a red notebook. He used green for his math materials.

Michael can still grab his materials in a hurry. It is easy to find two red things or two green things. Michael is doing much better now.

Get A School Map

In some schools, different classes are taught by different teachers. Students go to one room for reading, another for math, and another for social studies.

Some kids get confused about which room to go to for which class. A school map can help. If your school has a Parent Handbook, it may have a map you can copy. Or ask an adult to help you find or make a map.

Mark where your locker is on the map. Then color-code the classrooms you go to. If you use red for your reading materials, draw a red line around the reading room. Draw a red line from your locker to the reading room. Then, when you go to your locker, you can grab your reading materials and follow the red line to class.

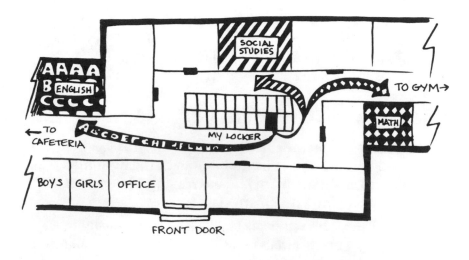

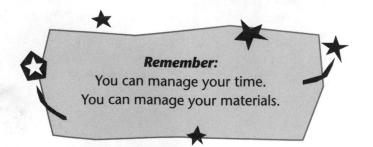

Remember:
You can manage your time.
You can manage your materials.

Chapter 2

Six Ways To Be A Better Learner

Sometimes students with LD try to answer questions or solve problems too quickly. They do not stop to think about what they are doing. They raise their hand before they are sure they know the answer. They rush through a worksheet without reading each question carefully. They will not ask for help with questions or problems they do not understand.

If you want to be a better learner, try some of the ideas in this chapter.

1. Stop, Listen, Look, Think

Some kids give up too soon on a question or problem. They take one look at it and decide they cannot answer or solve it.

Many times, they can do it if they *stop, listen* to the teacher, *look* at the question or problem again, and *think* about it. This gives your brain time to understand the question or problem.

STOP.   LISTEN.   LOOK.   THINK.

2. Read The Question Or Problem Out Loud

If you find a question or problem you do not understand, try reading it out loud. Hearing your voice say the question or problem may help your brain understand it.

A student named Korey was failing math. A test showed that he learned the least when he *saw* information. He learned the most when he *heard* it. His teacher let him take his math tests out in the hall. He could read the questions out loud to himself. Korey's grades went up. He stopped failing math.

3. Check For Mistakes

Try to finish assignments early so you have time to check for mistakes. Look for words that may be spelled wrong. Read your answers to see if they make sense. Read them out loud to make sure you have not left out important words.

4. Ask Yourself Questions

Many times, you will read materials you need to remember later for a test. Stop sometimes and ask yourself questions like these.

★ "Why am I reading this?"

★ "What is the main idea of this paragraph?"

★ "Who is the main character in this story?"

★ "When does this story take place?"

★ "What things will I need to remember for the test?"

5. Ask The Teacher Questions

If you do not understand something your teacher says, ask the teacher to explain. What if you do not want to do this in front of the class? Write down as much as you can of what the teacher says. Then ask the teacher to explain later.

Your teacher cannot read your mind. The only way your teacher can know that you do not understand something is if you speak up.

6. Use Memory Tricks

Try these or make up your own.

 Think of a silly picture to help you remember a paragraph you just read.

★ Repeat the spelling of a word ten times.

★ Make up words using the first letters of words you need to remember. For example: "All Mammals Are Furry" can become "AMAF." Learn "AMAF" and it will remind you that "All Mammals Are Furry." Here is another example: "All Birds Lay Eggs" can become "ABLE."

Do you need to learn the colors of the spectrum? They are Red, Orange, Yellow, Green, Blue, Indigo, and Violet. Their first letters make the name, "ROY G. BIV." Remember the name. It will help you to remember the colors.

★ Make up sayings using the first letters of words you need to remember. For example: You are learning the notes on the musical staff. The notes in the spaces are F, A, C, and E. They make the word "FACE." The notes on the lines are E, G, B, D, and F. You could remember the saying, "Every Good Bird Does Fly."

Draw pictures to go with the new words and sayings you make up.

Remember:
You can stop, listen, look, and think.
You can read a problem or question out loud.
You can ask questions.
You can use memory tricks.

Chapter 3

You Can Learn In Different Ways

Some people think that reading is the only way to learn. This is not true. Some kids learn by reading. Others learn by listening. Others learn by touching and moving.

Remember that LD means "learning different." Everyone learns in their own way. If you need different ways to learn, try some of the ideas in this chapter.

Use A Tape Recorder

There are many ways you can use a tape recorder to learn. If you have your own tape recorder, see if you can bring it to class. Or ask the teacher if you can borrow a tape recorder to use. You will need it at school and at home.

Here are three ways you might use a tape recorder. Can you think of more?

1. If it is hard to understand the teacher in class

Turn the tape recorder on when the teacher is talking. Later, when you get home, you can listen to what the teacher said. You can listen as many times as you want. You can stop the tape and write down important things.

2. If it is hard for you to learn by reading

Ask your teacher, parent, or another helper to record your reading assignments. Then you can learn by listening instead of reading. Better yet, read along while you listen to the tape.

3. If you are learning new spelling words

Read your spelling words into the tape recorder. Read each word and spelling, like this: "Tiger. T-I-G-E-R. Tiger." Copy the word two times on paper. Say it again. Spell it out loud.

Color-Code Your Materials

Mark important information in books or worksheets. Do it yourself, or ask a helper to do it for you. Use stick-on colored dots or highlighters (colored markers).

Red could mark the main ideas of paragraphs. Green could mark important facts. Yellow could mark new words. Black could mark information that is not important.

Write in your notebook what the colors mean.

Draw Pictures

There are many ways you can learn by drawing pictures. Here are two ideas to try.

1. When you are reading

If what you are reading makes you think of a picture, draw it. This will help you remember what you have read.

You might want to make a picture outline of what you are reading. For example: To remember this paragraph, you might draw a board.

John heard his dog bark loudly out by the hen house. John went out the door and started across the yard to the hen house. He picked up a board to use in case he needed to defend himself.

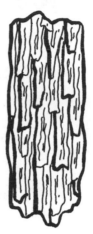

2. When you are studying for a test

Draw pictures of important ideas, people, or dates. Then, when you take the test, think of the pictures you drew.

Learn To Type Or Use A Computer

Do you have trouble writing clearly? Some kids with LD have learned to type. They do their work on a typewriter or a computer. Some of these students say they can think better when they type than when they write by hand. (Many people who do not have LD feel the same way.) You will find out more about computers in the next chapter.

Keep A Journal

Every day or week, take some time to write down your thoughts and feelings. Keep your journal in a notebook. Mark the notebook PRIVATE.

You can write in your journal any way you want. You can write anything you want. You do not have to worry about spelling or writing clearly. Your journal is just for you.

Keep writing in your journal for a long time. Every once in a while, look back to the beginning. You may find that your thinking, writing, and spelling are getting better.

Remember:
You can use a tape recorder.
You can draw pictures.
You can learn to type or use a computer.
You can keep a journal.

Chapter 4

You Can Use A Computer

Some kids with LD are better at using computers than kids without LD. Computers can be good friends. They do not get angry when you make a mistake. They wait patiently while you try to answer a question or understand a problem. They let you correct mistakes easily. And computers can be fun!

Eight Ways To Use A Computer

What can you do with a computer? Almost anything you want. There are many computer programs to try. If your school has computers, it probably has hundreds of computer programs. Many public libraries have computer programs you can check out.

1. Learn to type.

Some programs teach you how to type. You learn to find the right letters by touch, without looking at the keyboard. The more you practice, the faster you can type. This is a fine skill to learn. It is much easier to use the computer when you know how to type.

2. Do your writing.

Write book reports and stories. Write answers to questions or word problems. When you finish writing on the computer, print out what you have written. Read it over to check for mistakes. Mark your mistakes and correct them on the computer. Then print out a fresh new copy.

Programs called "spell checkers" can find and fix spelling mistakes for you.

3. Practice writing sentences.

Ask a teacher or parent to write mixed-up sentences on the computer. Then put the words in the right order to make real sentences.

4. Publish a newspaper.

Some programs let you print out newspapers with columns, headlines, even pictures. Would you like to publish a newspaper about your family or class? Maybe you can do this for a school assignment.

5. Play computer games.

Many computer games can help you to learn. There are math games, spelling games, history games, and more. They make learning fun.

6. Experience new things.

Special programs called "simulations" can let you try new experiences. You can be a pilot or an astronaut. You can be a member of a pioneer family traveling from Missouri to Oregon.

Simulation

SIM yə LĀ shən

7. Be an artist.

Some computer programs let you draw pictures or make designs. Use them to explore your talent as an artist.

8. Practice your facts.

Drill-and-practice programs can help you learn facts. There are programs for spelling facts, grammar facts, and math facts.

How To Get Computer Time

There are many ways you can use a computer to learn. But first, you have to get some computer time. This is not always easy to do.

Some teachers use computers to reward students who finish their work first or have the best behavior. In some schools, all of the computers are kept in a special room. Only certain students can go there and use the computers.

It can be hard for kids with LD to get computer time. This is too bad, since we know how much computers can help. If you want to use a school computer and you cannot get any computer time, try these ideas.

Talk to your parent.

Say that you need some computer time. Ask if your parent can talk to your teacher or principal about this.

Talk to your teacher.

Ask your classroom teacher or LD teacher how you can get some computer time. If you do not know how to use a computer, you will need someone to help you learn. Maybe your teacher can find a computer partner for you.

Stick up for your right to get computer time.

You have talked to your parent. You have talked to your teacher. You still cannot get computer time. What next?

You have a right to use the computers at your school. You can stick up for your right. Go to your school counselor or principal, and talk to that person yourself. Explain how a computer can help you learn. You could say, "If I can get computer time, my school work will improve. It will be easier for me to write assignments. I will not make as many mistakes. I will learn facts better and faster."

Maybe you cannot get computer time during school. What about after school?

Some schools will let students use the computers at the end of the day, after school is over. Find out if you can get computer time this way.

Maybe you cannot get computer time at school. Or maybe there are no computers at your school. Don't give up!

Other places may have computers you can use. What about the public library? What about a computer lab at a college? Some copy shops have computers you can use for short times. Some stores that sell computers also rent them. Keep looking. You will find a computer you can use.

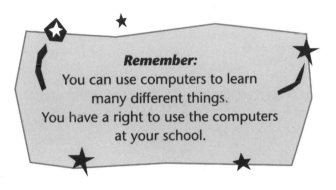

Remember:
You can use computers to learn
many different things.
You have a right to use the computers
at your school.

Chapter 5

You Can Manage Mainstreaming

Many kids with LD have two classrooms. One has lots of students and a regular teacher. The other has fewer students and a special kind of teacher.

The second kind of classroom is usually called a "resource room." (It may have a different name at your school.) This is where kids with LD get special help with their school work.

Resource room

RĒ sors rōŏm

Some kids with LD may be in the resource room for only part of the school day. Others may be there all day long. They will leave only to go to music, gym, and art. Some schools do not have resource rooms. Students with LD get special help in the regular classroom.

When a kid with LD spends all or part of the day in a regular classroom, this is called "mainstreaming."

Mainstreaming
MĀN strēm ing

Sometimes it can be embarrassing to leave your classroom to go to the resource room. Other kids may ask where you are going and why. You may not want to answer.

Other kids might tease you about going to the resource room. You might have to leave the regular classroom right in the middle of an activity. Or you might come back right when everyone else is busy doing something. Either way can feel funny.

Sherill is a friend of ours with LD. She says, "My second grade class was always listening to a story when I came back from the resource room. When I walked in, the teacher would stop reading. The kids would all look at me."

Tad is another friend of ours with LD. He says, "I went to the resource room for reading. When I came back, the other kids would be working on their math. The teacher would have to tell me what to do. She didn't seem very happy about it."

Even if you do not go to a resource room, you might get teased. Because you have LD, you learn differently from other kids. Some people tease anyone who dresses, talks, looks, or acts differently from them.

If you are having problems with mainstreaming, try some of the ideas in this chapter.

How To Answer Questions

What should you do when other kids ask questions? Like, "Where are you going?" Or, "Why do you go to the resource room?" Or, "What do you do there?" Or, "Why are you reading Book Three? Everybody else is reading Book Four."

You can choose to answer or not. It is up to you.

Some kids will not quit bugging you. You may want to answer them just so they will stop asking. The best answers are simple, honest answers.

Examples

WHEN SOMEONE ASKS:	YOU COULD SAY:
"Where are you going?"	"I'm going to the resource room."
"Why?"	"Because I want to," or "Because it's fun."
"What do you do there?"	"I learn stuff. It's no big deal."
"Why are you still in Book Three?"	"I am reading Book Three now. Then I will read Book Four."

How To Handle Teasing

Everyone gets teased in school. You may get teased about going to the resource room. You may get teased about the kind of school work you do.

You cannot control the kids who tease you. But you can control what you do when they tease you.

In our first book, *The Survival Guide For Kids With LD*, we wrote a chapter called, "What To Do When Other Kids Tease You." Here are three things we think are good to do.

Very Helpful Things To Do When You Get Teased

WHAT YOU CAN DO

Stand up straight and look the kid in the eye. Say in a calm voice, "I do not like to be talked to that way." Then walk away.

Talk to an adult you like and trust. Pick a person who is a good listener and who cares about you. Tell that person about the teasing and how you feel.

Do not tease others.

WHAT MIGHT HAPPEN

Even if the teasing does not stop, you will feel good about sticking up for yourself. And you will not get in trouble for fighting.

The kid teasing you may see that he or she cannot make you cry or get angry. The kid may give up trying.

You may have to repeat this many times before the kid "gets it." But that is still better than fighting or hiding your feelings.

You will feel better! No one can make kids stop teasing. But you can talk about your feelings, and that always helps.

You are a lot less likely to be teased if you do not tease.

How To Get Help

If you feel embarrassed about going to the resource room, tell your teacher. Ask if you, your regular teacher, and your resource room teacher can have a meeting. Try to solve this problem together.

What if the other kids are always working on something when you come back? Ask your teacher if someone else can tell you about the assignment and what to do.

Maybe your teacher can get a volunteer to help you. Many kids like to volunteer. It makes them feel important. If another student is helping you, both of you will feel special. Neither of you will feel funny.

What if other kids tease you? Remember that you cannot control them. But you can control what you do when they tease you.

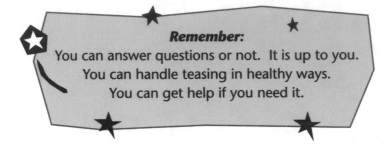

Remember:
You can answer questions or not. It is up to you.
You can handle teasing in healthy ways.
You can get help if you need it.

Chapter 6

You Can Handle Testing

Kids with LD get tested a lot! To you, it may seem like you are always being tested. You are always being pulled out of class. You are always taking the same test, over and over again.

Testing helps your teachers to learn more about you. It tells them if you are learning in school. It tells them if you need more special help with your school work.

You may not like being tested. But you can handle it. You can know about the people who do the testing. You can try some of the testing tips in this chapter.

Who Does The Testing?

Many different people test kids with LD. Here are some people you may have met along the way.

The school psychologist

Psychologist
sī KOL ə gist

A psychologist is a person who studies the mind and how it works. Your school or district may have a psychologist. This person probably tested you before you got into the LD program.

Do you remember the tests? You may have copied shapes on cards, or put blocks together to match pictures. Maybe you put pictures in order to tell a story, or repeated numbers.

The psychologist will test you about every three years. Or you could go for tests more often than that.

The speech therapist

Therapist

THER ə pist

A speech therapist is a person who studies the way people talk and understand what they hear. Your school or district may have a speech therapist. This person may be called something else at your school.

The speech therapist may ask you to say words. The therapist may say a word and ask you to point to a picture of that word.

The school nurse

The nurse will check to make sure that your eyes and ears are working okay. Most kids in your school will also take these tests.

The LD teacher or reading teacher

A special teacher will test you in school subjects like reading, writing, spelling, and math. In some schools, this will be the LD teacher. It may be someone different at your school.

Testing Truths

Most people who test kids try to make test time fun. They want you to feel comfortable. But some of the tests will be hard. They may not seem like fun to you.

You should know that many of these tests are different from other tests you take in school. On some of these tests, it is impossible to get everything right. But you have to keep going until you start to miss a lot. You may feel like you are doing badly. You are not. You are doing just what you are supposed to do.

Also, many of these tests are made for students of different ages. You could be 9 years old, taking the same test as someone 16 years old.

Some tests are meant to be taken more than once. You may take the same test two times in two years, or many times in many years. Do not worry about this. It is a way to keep track of how you are doing.

Five Tips For Handling Testing

1. Try to have a say about when you will be tested.

Every time Ariel was tested, she had to leave her computer class. This was her favorite class. She did not like to miss it all the time. So she asked her teacher if she could be tested at a different time.

2. Ask questions.

You have a right to ask questions about a test. Here are some questions you may want to ask.

★ "Why am I being tested?"

★ "What are you trying to find out with this test?"

★ "Is this a timed test?"

★ "How long will the test take?"

3. Do your best.

Some kids get so tired of tests that they stop trying. Then the testing does not do any good. It is just a big waste of time. Even if you get tired of tests, keep trying.

4. Keep your cool.

It is easy to get upset about a test, especially when you start to get a lot wrong. If you are feeling upset, tell the person who is testing you. Maybe you can take a break or talk for a while.

5. Find out how you did on the test.

You have a right to know how you did. The person who tested you should be glad to talk to you about the results. But be patient. This may not happen right away. It usually takes one to two weeks to score your tests. (Sometimes it takes longer.)

Do not ask to know the answers to questions on the test. For example, do not ask, "Did I get number eight right?" Or, "Did I get the math question right?" Most tests have rules about this. The person testing you cannot give out the answers to questions.

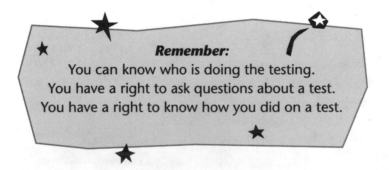

Remember:
You can know who is doing the testing.
You have a right to ask questions about a test.
You have a right to know how you did on a test.

Chapter 7

You Can Master Time

Rhoda used to teach seventh grade history. One year, she had a student with LD named Courtney. Like the other students, Courtney went to a different classroom for each subject. Everyone had five minutes to get from one class to another.

One day Rhoda was walking down the hall between classes. The hall was crowded with students. Suddenly Rhoda saw Courtney running down the hall. Courtney had a worried look on her face. Rhoda stopped her.

"Why are you running?" Rhoda asked Courtney. "You have almost five minutes to get to your next class. And it's just around the corner."

Courtney said, "I know that I have five minutes. But I still have to hurry because I don't know how much time five minutes really is."

Years later, when Courtney was in college, she still got to her classes earlier than the other students. Because she did not understand time, she sometimes went to places a whole hour or two early. She was always afraid that she would be late.

Many kids with LD have trouble understanding time. They can read a digital clock (the kind that has numbers instead of hands), but they do not understand what it means.

If you have trouble with time, try some of the ideas in this chapter.

Which Takes Longer?

Ask someone to help you learn about time. This can be your classroom teacher, your LD teacher, a parent, or another adult. It can be a big brother or sister or friend.

Have your helper name two events, like taking out the garbage and cleaning your room. Tell which one takes longer.

Now have your helper make a list of many events. Number them, starting with the one that takes the least amount of time. When you are finished, show the list to your helper. Ask if your helper agrees with your numbers.

2 Eating dinner

4 Cleaning your room

5 Watching a movie

1 Washing your hands

3 Walking to school

6 Spending the night at a friend's house

Use A Calendar

Write down important dates on a calendar. You might include your birthday and spring vacation. You might write the dates when your grandparents will visit.

As the year goes by, cross out each day. Think about how many days are left until your next birthday. Think about how many weeks are left. Think about how many months are left.

Learn Different Ways To Tell Time

Ask a helper to make cards showing the different ways to tell time. They should include a clock face with hands, a digital clock face, and time words spelled out.

9:25

Nine twenty·five

Have your helper make several cards showing each way. Go through the cards every day until you know the different ways to tell time.

"Clock" Your Day

Draw blank clock faces on index cards. Think about all the things you will do today. Mark the times on the clocks.

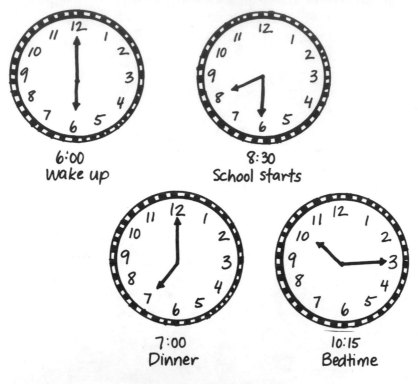

6:00
Wake up

8:30
School starts

7:00
Dinner

10:15
Bedtime

Make A Clock Game

You will need a paper plate, cardboard, scissors, a round-head paper fastener, and index cards.

Draw a blank clock face on the paper plate. Cut out an hour hand and a minute hand from cardboard. Attach the hands to the clock face with the paper fastener.

Ask a helper to write different times on the index cards. Place the cards face down in front of you. Draw a card and move the clock hands to show the time.

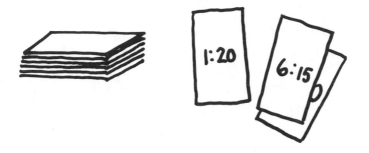

Practice "In" And "Ago"

Ask a helper to write problems like these on index cards.

Time shown: _____
20 minutes ago: _____

Time shown: _____
In 10 minutes: _____

Time shown: _____
5 minutes ago: _____

Time shown: _____
In 5 minutes: _____

Work these problems until you understand when someone says "in five minutes" or "20 minutes ago."

Travel Through Time

Do you know how much time it takes you to do things? Find out by trying these.

★ Tell your family that you are going to walk around the block. Say how long it is going to take. Check the clock before you go. Check the clock when you come back. How close did you come to guessing the time it would take?

★ Say that you are going to take a bath. Say that you will be in the bathtub for 20 minutes. Check the clock before you go into the bathroom. Do not take a clock or a watch in with you. When you think 20 minutes have passed, come out of the bathroom. Check the clock again. How close did you come to 20 minutes?

Think of other ways to check your feeling for time. Ask people to help you. It is important for you to understand time. Then you will not always be too early or too late.

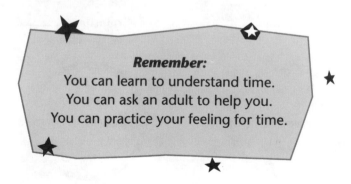

Remember:
You can learn to understand time.
You can ask an adult to help you.
You can practice your feeling for time.

Chapter 8

You Can Get Help From Adults

You are learning many ways to help yourself. Still, there will be times when you need to ask an adult for help.

This can be hard for anyone to do. It can be especially hard for kids with LD. You may be afraid that the adult will get mad at you or yell at you. You may worry that the adult will make fun of you or ignore you. It is true that some adults will not want to help you. But most will.

Know When To Ask For Help

There are some problems you can handle yourself. For others, you need help. How can you tell the difference? For each problem, ask yourself these two questions.

1. Have I tried my hardest?

You look at a math problem. It looks hard! At first you think you cannot solve it. But before you ask for help, take time to really study the problem. Make sure that you really cannot solve it.

 First, read the problem carefully. Then try to solve it. Write down all your steps.

 Now read the problem again. Look at how you tried to solve it. Can you change any of your steps?

 Read the problem one more time. Try to solve it one more time.

If you read the problem and try to solve it three times, and you still cannot do it, ask for help. You will be able to prove that you tried your best. The adult will be more willing to help you.

2. Am I going too fast?

Slow down. Count to 10. Think about the problem. Try to solve it yourself. Try three times. You might be surprised at how much you can do without asking for help.

Know Who To Ask For Help

You will face many kinds of problems in your life. School work may be hard. Other kids may tease you. A teacher may blame you for something you did not do. A parent may ground you. You may feel sad and lonely for a lot of different reasons.

You do not have to face your problems by yourself. There are many adults who can help you. Can you think of at least three adults you could ask for help? Here are some ideas.

Your mom or dad

Sometimes kids do not tell their parents when they have a problem. They think their parents will get mad at them or punish them. They worry that their parents are too busy to listen.

If you have a problem, try telling your parents first. If they act mad or yell, do not get mad or yell back. Try telling them a second time. If they still act mad or yell, give them time to calm down. Try again later.

If your parents are busy, ask them when would be a good time to talk. Tell them you really need to talk.

A teacher

Some teachers can help with many kinds of problems, not just school problems. Maybe you are not getting along with your parents. Maybe other students are teasing you, or you are feeling lonely. Try asking a teacher for help. Start with your classroom teacher or your LD teacher.

If your teachers are not very helpful, do not give up. Do you know another teacher in the building you can trust? Try asking that teacher for help.

Most teachers like kids and want to help them. A teacher may be the best friend you can have. But remember that teachers are busy and work hard. Do not take every single problem you have to a teacher. Try to think of ways to solve your own problems first.

The school counselor

Some schools have counselors. These people have been trained to help kids solve their problems. They listen and give advice.

Counselor
KOUN səl ər

Counselors are also trained to keep things "confidential." This means you can tell them almost anything, and they will not tell anyone else without your permission. They will not even tell your parents unless you say it is okay.

Confidential
kon fi DEN shəl

There are some things school counselors cannot keep confidential. For example, the law says they must tell if a young person is being hurt by adults. If you want to know what things your counselor must tell, ask. You should feel free to talk to the counselor about any problem you are having at school, at home, or inside yourself.

Not all schools have counselors. In some schools, a psychologist or a social worker helps kids with their problems. If your school does not have a counselor, psychologist, or social worker, do not give up. Talk to your teacher or principal. Explain that you need somebody to talk to.

Other adults you can trust

Sometimes you may not be able to talk to your parents or a teacher. You may not be able to talk to a counselor. Think about other adults you might be able to talk to.

What about your relatives? Grandparents are often the very best adults to talk to. (Sometimes they may seem to understand you better than your parents.) Other relatives, like aunts, uncles, and cousins, may be able to help. You may have an older brother or sister who will listen to you. Think of the people who love you. Do not be afraid to ask them for help.

Who are some other adults you can trust? A coach? A scout leader? A neighbor? (Make sure this is someone your parents know.) Could one of them help you? You will never know unless you ask.

There are many adults who will listen to you and help you if they can. Keep trying until you find someone who will help you.

Be Honest About Your LD

Rhoda met Sheila on the first day of the new school year. Sheila came up to Rhoda's desk right after class. She told Rhoda that she had LD.

"I have a hard time reading," Sheila said. "Sometimes when I read, the letters move around on the page. I can learn better if I sit close to the front. Also, can I bring a tape recorder to class? Then I can tape things I need to remember."

Sheila was honest about her LD. This helped Rhoda to know the best way to teach Sheila.

Sometimes students with LD are afraid or ashamed to talk about it. They do not want anyone else to know about their learning differences. They think other people will not like them if they know. Most adults will not like you any less (or any more) because you have LD. But knowing about it can help them to help you.

Know How To Ask For Help

Tell the adult ahead of time that you need to talk.

Remember that adults are often busy. Do not just start talking about your problem. Busy adults may not pay attention. Or they may get mad at you for interrupting.

Instead, say that you need to talk sometime soon. Ask, "When would be a good time for you?" Say you would like to sit down together in a quiet place.

They may stop what they are doing right then, or they may say, "I can talk to you in a few minutes." Or, "I can talk to you in an hour." If the time passes and they do not come to talk to you, they probably forgot. It is okay to remind them. Do not get angry. Just ask politely when they will be able to talk to you.

Start out the right way.

Admit that you have a problem. You could start by saying, "I have a problem I can't solve by myself. I trust you, and I need your help."

Do not just say, "I had to stay after school today." Or, "I failed my math test today." Or, "I hate Johnny." These kinds of statements only give bad news. They do not give the right kind of information. For adults to help you, they need to know why a thing happened, or why you feel the way you do. Did you have to stay after school because you got in trouble? Did you fail your math test because you did not understand the problems? Do you hate Johnny because he took your lunch money?

When you say, "I need your help," most adults will feel helpful. When you start out with bad news, most adults will feel worried. It is easy to go from feeling worried to feeling angry.

Always be calm and polite.

Even when it is hard, try to talk about your problem in a calm, polite way. Do not start yelling. Do not use bad words. If you yell or use bad words, the adult may not want to talk to you. You may not get any help with your problem.

If you start getting upset, tell the adult about it. Say, "I need a few minutes to calm down." Then take deep breaths or count to 10.

Be sure to listen.

When an adult agrees to listen to your problem, do not forget to listen back.

Maybe you have just told your father about a problem. He has listened to you. Now it is his turn to talk. Make sure that you listen to him. He may have good advice for you. Do not walk away or start talking about something else.

Sometimes kids like to do all the talking. They do not like to listen when adults talk to them. Remember: If you want help with a problem, you must be willing to listen, not only talk.

Know How To Use The Help You Get

Maybe your father gave you good advice. Now you must take it and make it work. Here are three ways to follow through.

1. Write it down.

If an adult gives you an idea for solving your problem, write it down. Or ask the adult to help you write it down. Then read it. Study it. Act it out in front of a mirror, or with someone you trust. Practice the solution until you can do it.

2. Try it out.

When you have practiced the solution, try it out. If it works, tell the adult who gave you the idea. If it does not work, tell the adult. Maybe you can come up with another solution.

3. Do not forget it.

In your journal, write about your problem and the solution. Every time you solve a problem, write about it. Every time you read your journal, it will remind you of how you solved problems in your life.

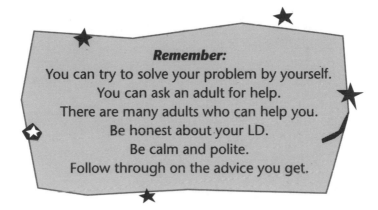

Remember:
You can try to solve your problem by yourself.
You can ask an adult for help.
There are many adults who can help you.
Be honest about your LD.
Be calm and polite.
Follow through on the advice you get.

PART TWO:

SCHOOL TOOLS FOR LEARNING

Chapter 9

Ten Ways To Be
A Better Reader

Many kids with LD have trouble with reading. Some say that the letters move around when they try to read. Some say that they cannot pay attention because there are too many words on the page. Others do not know why they have trouble with reading. They just do.

Some kids with LD think of ways to learn without having to read. There are many adults who cannot read well, but they are successful anyway. Cher has always had trouble with reading. So has Bruce Jenner, the Olympic gold medal winner.

If you cannot read well, do not give up on yourself. Try your hardest to be the best reader you can be. Never think of yourself as a "bad reader" or a "poor reader." Instead, think of yourself as a good person You will still grow up. You will still get along in the world. Who knows—you may even be famous someday!

Sometimes kids with LD are better readers than they think they are. They just need ideas to help them read. Here are some ideas that have helped kids we know.

1. Find A Quiet Place

Do not try to read when the TV is on. Do not try to read when people around you are talking. If you are in the classroom, ask the teacher to help you find a quiet place to read.

2. Use A Ruler Or Cardboard To Keep Your Place

Place a ruler under the line you are reading. This will help you keep your mind on each sentence as you read it.

Do you get distracted by the other letters on the page? Then use a piece of cardboard to cover the letters below the sentence you are reading.

3. Use Pictures

If there are pictures in what you are reading, be sure to look at them. They may give you clues about words you do not know.

Find a magazine with lots of pictures. When you finish a reading assignment, look through the magazine. Find three pictures that remind you of what you just read.

4. Make A Word Bank

When you see a word you do not know, ask your teacher or parent to say it for you and tell you what it means. Then you try to say it. When you can say the word and its meaning, write them on an index card. Put the card in a box. This is the start of your "word bank."

Now, every time you see a word you do not know, add it to your word bank. Practice saying, learning, and using the words. Ask someone to help you. This can be your classroom teacher, your LD teacher, a parent, or another adult. It can be a big brother or sister or friend.

When you have many words in your bank, ask your teacher if you can use them in a school assignment. Here are some ideas for assignments.

 Match the words with words in books or the newspaper.

 Make sentences with the words.

 Write a story using the words.

You can also use your word bank to be a better speller. Learn how on page 78.

5. Make Up A Story And Read It

Think of a story in your head. Ask a helper to type it for you while you tell it. After the story is typed, see if you can read it. Add the words you do not know to your word bank.

6. Use A Reading Guide

When you get a reading assignment, ask your teacher to make a "reading guide." This can point out important information. It can point out words you need to learn and remember. It can also point out parts you do not need to read and remember.

Here is an example of a reading guide.

Chap. 2

P. 61 — Look at the picture of the map on this page. Find the state of Nebraska. Find the city of Lincoln.

P. 65 — Paragraph 2. Pay attention to the term "export crop."

P. 68 — Paragraphs 5-8. Read this section carefully. You will need to remember this information for the test.

7. Share What You Read

Read something that is interesting to you. Remember what you read and share it with a teacher, parent, or friend.

8. Make Up Titles

Read an interesting paragraph. Or have a helper make up a paragraph and write it down. Read the paragraph and make up a title for it.

9. Take Notes

When you read, have a notebook and something to write with. Write down important ideas, dates, and "key words."

A key word can sum up a whole page of reading material. When you look over your notes later, a key word can "unlock" the material in your mind.

Here is an example of a page from a book, with key words you might write down.

There are 50 states in the United States of America. Hawaii was the last state to be added. The people who live in Hawaii represent many different cultures. They all live and work together in a cooperative way.

The climate in Hawaii is mild, although snow sometimes falls on the highest mountains. There are many active volcanoes in Hawaii. Lava from these volcanoes spills out onto the land and into the ocean, so that the size and shape of the Hawaiian Islands continue to grow and change.

10. Read For Fun

The *best* way to get better at reading is to read as much as you can. So turn off the TV and READ! Read books about things you like. Read comic books, cartoon books, and magazines. Listen to a book on tape and read along while you listen. Read the funnies in the newspaper.

Ask your LD teacher for a list of books to read. See if you can find them at your school library. Or visit your public library. If you do not have a library card, get one of your own.

The more you read, the easier reading will become. The more you read, the less trouble you will have with reading.

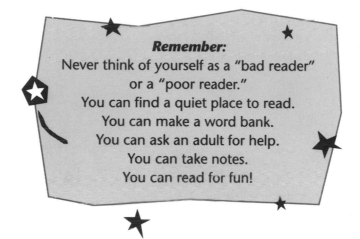

Remember:
Never think of yourself as a "bad reader"
or a "poor reader."
You can find a quiet place to read.
You can make a word bank.
You can ask an adult for help.
You can take notes.
You can read for fun!

Chapter 10
Ten Steps To Better Writing

To do well in school, you have to do a lot of writing. Even if you know how to type, there are times when you cannot use a typewriter or a computer. You have to write by hand.

Sometimes writing is hard for kids with LD. Maybe you know in your head what you want to write about. But when you try to write it down, you make mistakes. Maybe it is hard for you to hold your pencil in the right way. Maybe you cannot keep your paper still while you write. Maybe you erase so much that your paper looks terrible. Some kids erase so much, they put holes in their paper! If your papers are hard to read, or if they have many mistakes, you may get low grades.

If you would like to write better, try some of the ideas in this chapter.

1. Practice Writing Movements

Spend some time each day just using a pencil to make shapes. Draw circles, squares, letters, and numbers. Make lots of circles. Make lots of squares. Write each letter from A to Z five times. Write each number from 1 to 10 five times.

Be a doodler. Draw shapes when you are talking to friends on the phone. Draw letters when you are watching TV. Draw numbers when you are listening to music.

Use different materials to practice writing movements. Try finger paints. Write in a tray filled with sand, cornmeal, or flour.

Write a letter on a friend. (Not TO a friend, ON a friend.) Use your finger to trace a letter on a friend's back. Have your friend guess the letter.

2. Use Correct Posture

Sit up straight in a comfortable chair. Keep both feet flat on the floor. Place both arms on the table or desk. Place the hand you do not write with at the top of the paper, to keep it from moving.

3. Keep Your Paper Straight

If you write with your right hand, tilt the paper slightly to the left. If you write with your left hand, tilt it slightly to the right.

Do you have trouble remembering the right slant? Ask your parent or teacher to place a strip of tape slanting the right way at the top of your table or desk. Use the tape as a guide to help you place your paper the right way.

Does your paper move around when you try to write? Place a piece of masking tape at the top of the paper to keep it still. Removable tape works well, too.

4. Hold Your Pencil Or Pen The Right Way

Hold your pencil between your thumb and middle finger. Place your index finger (your first finger) on top of the pencil or pen. Your thumb and index finger should be just above the point.

Is it hard to remember the right place to hold the pencil? Put a rubber band around the pencil at the place where you should hold it.

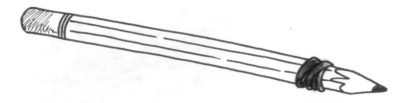

Is the pencil or pen too skinny for you to hold easily? Slide it through a foam or rubber ball. Then place your thumb and fingers around the ball to practice the right grip.

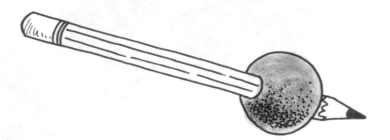

Or get a "finger grip." These are made of colorful plastic or rubber. They slide over the pencil and make it easier to hold. They do not cost much money—less than $1.00. Maybe your teacher has one you can borrow.

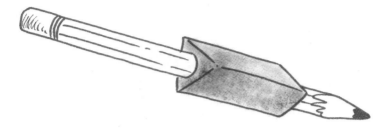

Do not use short pencils. They are too hard to hold.

5. Practice With Stencils

Get a stencil sheet with letters and numbers. Clip it to a piece of paper. Use a pencil, a colored marker, or a crayon to trace the letters and numbers. Remove the stencil sheet to see what you have made. Then try writing the letters and numbers without the stencil sheet.

6. Try Tracing

Ask a helper to write big, black letters and numbers on a sheet of paper. Clip a sheet of see-through paper over it. Use a felt-tipped pen to trace over the letters and numbers. Then try writing them without tracing them.

7. Draw Between The Lines

Ask a helper to draw big, open shapes for you. Here are some examples.

Draw between the lines of the shapes. This will give you practice controlling your pencil.

On page 151, you will find letters to practice with. Make a copy of that page. Then draw between the lines of each letter. Use numbers to show the order you drew your lines in. Use arrows to show the direction of each line. Here is an example.

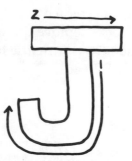

8. Do Dot-To-Dots

Ask your classroom teacher or LD teacher to draw big letters and dotted outlines. Here are some examples.

Connect the dots to make the letters. Then try writing the letters without the dots.

9. Use Lined Paper

Use paper with solid and dotted lines to practice placing letters the right way.

One-line letters go between the two solid lines.

Two-line letters go between the top solid line and the bottom dotted line.

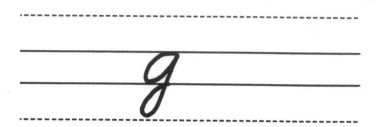

Or they go between the bottom solid line and the top dotted line.

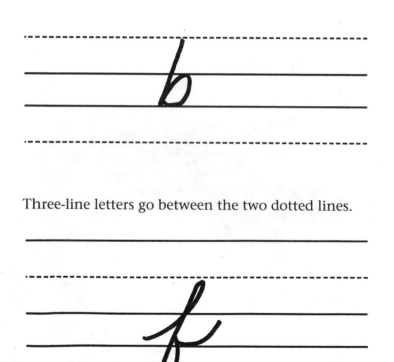

Three-line letters go between the two dotted lines.

10. Copy Words From A Book

Open a book to any page. Copy every other word by writing it in cursive. (Or you can copy every third word, or every fourth word.)

Keep practicing. The more you write, the better your writing may get. It will not be so hard for you to write.

Remember:
Use correct posture.
Keep your paper straight.
Hold your pencil or pen the right way.
Practice, practice, practice!

Chapter 11

Eight Ways To Be A Better Speller

Lots of people who do not have LD cannot spell well. So if you have trouble spelling, do not feel bad. This is one of the easiest problems to solve.

There are many ways you can help yourself be a better speller. Here are some of our favorite ways.

1. Use Your Senses

Do not just read the word silently to yourself. Use as many of your senses as you can.

 LOOK at the word. Say it. Use it in a sentence.

 SEE the word. Look at the word. Close your eyes and "see" it in your mind. Say the word. Use it in a sentence.

77

★ SAY the word. Say it out loud. Spell it out loud.
Use it in a sentence.

★ HEAR the word. Listen to yourself say it out loud.
Listen to yourself spell it. Listen to yourself use it
in a sentence.

★ FEEL the word. Ask a helper to write it in big
letters. Trace it with your finger, and say it out loud
at the same time. Write the word without looking
at it. Spell it out loud. Use the word in a sentence.

2. Make A Word Bank

Every time you learn to spell a new word, write it on an
index card or a slip of paper. Put it in a box. This is the start
of your "word bank."

Once a week, take all the words out of your word bank.
Say and spell each word out loud.

Ask your teacher if you can use your words in a school
assignment. Here are some ideas for assignments.

★ Make sentences with the words.

★ Write a story using the words.

You can also use your word bank to be a better reader.
Learn how on pages 62–63.

3. Make Crossword Puzzles

Make crossword puzzles with new spelling words. On page 152, you will find a "Crossword Puzzle" form to copy and use.

4. Make A Dictionary

You will need 26 sheets of notebook paper, a notebook, and something to write with.

On each sheet of paper, write a letter of the alphabet in the upper right-hand corner. Begin with A and end with Z. Put all of the sheets in the notebook, in order. This is the start of your "dictionary."

Now, whenever you learn a new word, write it in your dictionary. Write words starting with "A" on the A page, and so on.

5. Fill In The Letters

   Ask a helper to write your spelling words in a special way. Each word should have one letter missing. Fill in the missing letters.

6. Make A Word Search Puzzle

   Use graph paper to make a word search puzzle. Ask your teacher for some graph paper.

   Write your spelling words on the graph paper. Write them in different places. Write them in different ways.

	G	I	R	A	F	F	E	
							T	
		M			N			
		I		E		R		
		R	R			O		
		R				C		
		O				K		
S	T	R	I	N	G			

Now fill in the rest of the squares with letters.

R	G	I	R	A	F	F	E	T
X	M	N	C	B	L	R	T	W
F	E	M	D	S	Q	N	B	X
C	G	I	K	M	E	A	R	P
S	T	R	E	R	M	W	O	Z
O	P	R	X	L	R	S	C	E
G	M	O	A	L	P	G	K	R
S	T	R	I	N	G	E	S	A

Ask your friends to make word search puzzles using the same spelling words. Exchange your puzzles. Have fun finding the words.

7. Practice Writing Spelling Words

This is not as much fun as puzzles, but it works. Write each spelling word five times. If you are still not sure how to spell a word, write it five more times. Keep writing it until you know it by heart.

8. Use A Special Dictionary

Remember that many people cannot spell well. In fact, there are so many poor spellers that special dictionaries have been made.

With most dictionaries, you have to know how a word is spelled before you can look it up. Not with these special dictionaries. You look up a word any way you think it is spelled. The dictionary tells you the right spelling.

For example: You want to know the right spelling of the word "juice." You think it might be spelled "joose." Or maybe it is spelled "juce." You look up both spellings. Next to each one is the right spelling, "juice."

joose	juice
juce	juice

Special dictionaries can be very handy! One is called:

 How To Spell It: A Dictionary of Commonly Misspelled Words by Harriet Wittels and Joan Greisman (New York: Grosset & Dunlap, 1973).

Maybe you can find it in your library. Or maybe your teacher has a copy you can use. If you want to buy your own copy, it costs about $10.00.

Another special dictionary is called:

 The Bad Speller's Dictionary by J. Krevisky and J. Linfield (New York: Random House, 1963).

This dictionary also has words that sound alike but are spelled differently. It gives you the right meaning for each word. Here is an example.

To	(Toward)
Too	(Also)
Two	(Number)

You can make your own special dictionary. Have a helper read your spelling words aloud. Write down the way you think each word is spelled. Then check your spelling list. If you spelled a word right, give yourself a star. If you spelled it wrong, write down the right spelling.

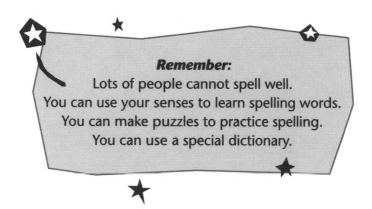

Remember:
Lots of people cannot spell well.
You can use your senses to learn spelling words.
You can make puzzles to practice spelling.
You can use a special dictionary.

Chapter 12

How To Solve Your Math Problems

For many students with LD, math is the hardest subject to learn. They do not understand what all those numbers mean. They get confused because numbers are used in many different ways. Adding, subtracting, multiplying, dividing, fractions—it is easy to get confused!

If you have trouble with math, tell your classroom teacher or LD teacher. Maybe there is a different way to teach you. Or maybe you can use a different math book. Remember that you learn differently. Whatever works for you is okay.

You can help yourself to do better in math. Try the ideas in this chapter. If you find one you do not understand, ask someone to help you. This can be your classroom teacher, your LD teacher, a parent, or another adult. It can be a big brother or sister or friend.

Get The Facts

Memorizing math facts can be boring. Almost nobody likes to do it. But math gets much easier when you "get the facts."

Try to memorize as many math facts as you can. Write them down. Say them out loud. Play games with them. Practice them with friends. Try to learn a new math fact every day.

Use Graph Paper

Some kids get the wrong answers in math because they cannot keep the numbers lined up the right way. Maybe they add numbers in the 10's column to numbers in the 1's column.

Graph paper can help you keep numbers straight. Ask your teacher for some graph paper.

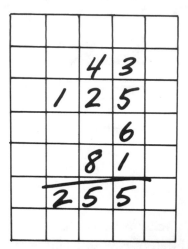

Learn The Signal Words

What does it mean to "find the sum"? It means that you will be *adding* numbers. "Sum" is a "signal word." A signal word tells you what to do with the numbers in a math problem.

You can make a chart of signal words. Put the chart in your math notebook. Use it when you do story problems.

Sum	⟶	+ Answer
Difference	⟶	− Answer
Product	⟶	x Answer
Quotient	⟶	÷ Answer

Add other signal words as you learn them.

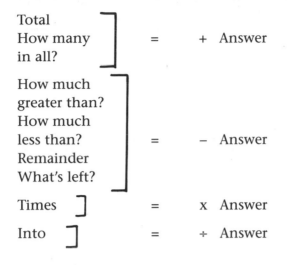

Total / How many / in all?	=	+ Answer
How much greater than? / How much less than? / Remainder / What's left?	=	− Answer
Times	=	x Answer
Into	=	÷ Answer

Addition Helpers

1. Make a model for "turn-arounds."

Sometimes teachers use big words when they talk about math. Maybe you have heard the word "commutative."

Commutative

kə MYŌŌ tə tiv

This is a hard word with an easy meaning. All it means is, when you add numbers, the sum is the same even if you change the order. You can "turn the numbers around" and the sum is the same.

EXAMPLE

$$2 + 3 = 5$$
$$3 + 2 = 5$$

In the example, it does not matter which comes first, the 2 or the 3. The sum is the same.

You can make a model to show this. Write a math problem on the front of an index card. Write the "turn-around" problem on the back. Put paper clips on the card. See for yourself that addition is commutative.

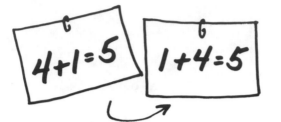

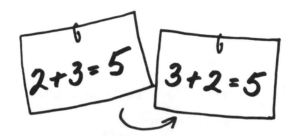

2. Learn addition doubles.

Look at the chart on page 89. Use it to learn addition doubles.

ADDITION DOUBLES

Double	Look	Listen

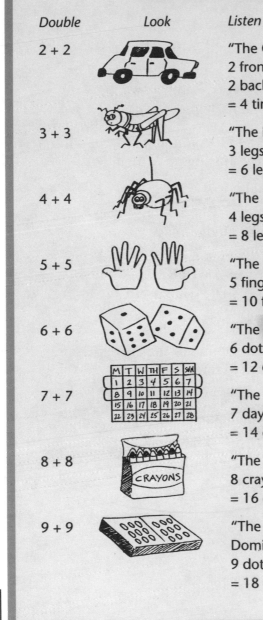

2 + 2 — "The Car Fact"
2 front tires
2 back tires
= 4 tires

3 + 3 — "The Bug Fact"
3 legs on each side
= 6 legs

4 + 4 — "The Spider Fact"
4 legs on each side
= 8 legs

5 + 5 — "The Fingers Fact"
5 fingers on each hand
= 10 fingers

6 + 6 — "The Dice Fact"
6 dots on each die
= 12 dots

7 + 7 — "The Two Weeks Fact"
7 days in each week
= 14 days

8 + 8 — "The Crayon Fact"
8 crayons in each row
= 16 crayons

9 + 9 — "The Double-Nine
Dominoes Fact"
9 dots on each side
= 18 dots

3. Learn the numbers that add up to 10.

Copy these problems for your notebook.

$$5 + 5 = 10$$
$$6 + 4 = 10$$
$$7 + 3 = 10$$
$$8 + 2 = 10$$
$$9 + 1 = 10$$

Remember that addition is commutative. You can turn the numbers around and they still add up to 10.

4. Learn "plus-9" facts.

FACT: 9 + (any number) is always 1 less than 10 + (that number).

EXAMPLE

9 + 4 is 1 less than 10 + 4

10 + 4 = 14, so 9 + 4 = 13

FACT: The digit in the 1's column of the answer is always 1 less than the digit added to the 9.

EXAMPLES

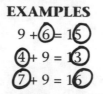

$$9 + 6 = 15$$
$$4 + 9 = 13$$
$$7 + 9 = 16$$

5. Relate hard facts to easy facts.

TIP: Think of doubles.

EXAMPLE

5 + 6 = ?

5 + 5 = 10, so 5 + 6 is 1 more

5 + 6 = 11

TIP: Think of the numbers that add up to 10.

EXAMPLE

7 + 4 = ?

7 + 3 = 10, so 7 + 4 is 1 more

7 + 4 = 11

6. Learn new ways to solve problems.

How do you solve addition problems where you have to carry? Maybe you learned just one way. But there are many ways to solve these problems. Another way is by finding partial sums.

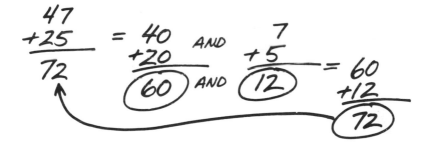

Ask your teacher to show you more ways to solve addition problems.

Subtraction Helpers

1. Memorize addition facts.

Did you learn the numbers that add up to 10? Then you already know many subtraction facts.

EXAMPLE

If you know that $6 + 4 = 10$

Then you know that $10 - 6 = 4$

And you know that $10 - 4 = 6$

If you know that $3 + 7 = 10$, what two subtraction facts do you know?

2. Add to check your answers.

$$\begin{array}{r} 7 \\ -3 \\ \hline 4 \end{array} \qquad \begin{array}{r} 4 \\ +3 \\ \hline 7 \end{array}$$

$$\begin{array}{r} 9 \\ -4 \\ \hline 5 \end{array} \qquad \begin{array}{r} 5 \\ +4 \\ \hline 9 \end{array}$$

$$\begin{array}{r} 5 \\ -1 \\ \hline 4 \end{array} \qquad \begin{array}{r} 4 \\ +1 \\ \hline 5 \end{array}$$

92

3. Use your pointer finger to subtract through 10.

Look at the index finger of your right hand. Maybe you call this your "pointer finger." Pretend that your fingernail is a zero. (You can even write a zero on it to help you remember.) Use your zero finger to help solve subtraction problems.

EXAMPLE

Cover the 1's digit with your zero finger. Now this problem looks like a 10's problem. Subtract from 10 and add the extras.

Multiplication Helpers

Like addition, multiplication is commutative. You can multiply numbers in any order and the product is the same.

1. "Finger" the 9's tables.

You can use your hands to multiply 9's. Start by numbering your fingers.

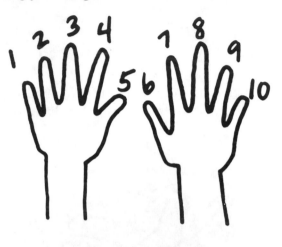

EXAMPLE

Multiply 9 x 3 (or 3 x 9)

STEP 1: Fold down the finger that is the smallest number. (In this example, the 3 finger.)

STEP 2: Count the number of fingers to the LEFT of the folded finger. The answer is 2.

STEP 3: Count the number of fingers to the RIGHT of the folded finger. The answer is 7.

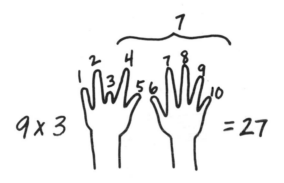

STEP 4: Put the numbers together. The answer to the problem 9 x 3 = 27.

Multiply 9 x 7 (or 7 x 9)

Fold down finger 7. There are 6 fingers to the left and 3 fingers to the right. The answer is 63.

2. Learn your 9's another way.

Study these problems and products:

$$9 \times 9 = 81$$
$$9 \times 8 = 72$$
$$9 \times 7 = 63$$
$$9 \times 6 = 54$$
$$9 \times 5 = 45$$
$$9 \times 4 = 36$$
$$9 \times 3 = 27$$
$$9 \times 2 = 18$$

Can you see a pattern? The number in the 10's place is always one smaller than the number you are multiplying by.

EXAMPLE

9 x 6 = 54 (the 5 is one smaller than 6)

What happens when you add the two numbers in the product together? The sum is always 9.

EXAMPLES

$9 \times 5 = 45 \ (4 + 5 = 9)$

$9 \times 2 = 18 \ (1 + 8 = 9)$

Division Helpers

1. Memorize multiplication facts.

It helps to know your multiplication facts before you start learning division. Every time you learn a multiplication fact, you learn *two* division facts. Here is an example.

EXAMPLE

When you learn this:

$5 \times 7 = 35$

You also learn these:

$35 \div 5 = 7$ Division Fact #1

$35 \div 7 = 5$ Division Fact #2

2. Check your answers by multiplying.

Once you know your multiplication facts, you can check your answers to division problems.

EXAMPLES

$15 \div 3 = 5$ CHECK: $5 \times 3 = 15$

$28 \div 7 = 4$ CHECK: $4 \times 7 = 28$

3. Make puzzles to remember "fact families."

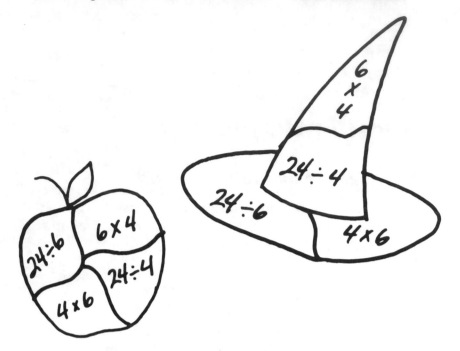

Fraction Helpers

Fraction problems are hard for most kids, not just kids with LD. Fractions are easier if you think about how you use them in real life. For example, "$\frac{1}{4}$" makes sense if you think about 1 apple cut into 4 equal pieces. Each piece is $\frac{1}{4}$ of the apple.

= 1 apple

= 1/4 apple

Or think about 3 jellybeans. You eat 2 and your little brother gets 1. You could say, "I ate 2 out of the 3 jellybeans." Your brother could say, "You got $\frac{2}{3}$ of the jellybeans, you creep, and I only got $\frac{1}{3}$."

What are some other ways you use fractions in your life? How would you divide 6 cookies so that you and your sister each got the same number? How would you split 1 soda with 2 of your friends? How would you share 1 foot-long hot dog with 4 kids on your soccer team? If you can think of ways to solve these problems, you can understand fractions.

1. Know the parts of a fraction.

Every fraction has an "upstairs number." Every fraction has a "downstairs number."

These have big names that sound alike. The upstairs number is the "numerator." The downstairs number is the "denominator."

Upstairs number➛ 3 ⬅Numerator

Downstairs number➛ 4 ⬅Denominator

Numerator
NŌŌ mə RĀ tər
Denominator
di NOM ə NĀ tər

TIP: "Denominator" and "Downstairs" both start with the letter D.

2. Use a grid to multiply fractions.

EXAMPLE

Find the answer to $\frac{2}{3}$ x $\frac{1}{2}$.

STEP 1: Multiply the denominators: 3 x 2 = 6

STEP 2: Draw a grid with that many squares.

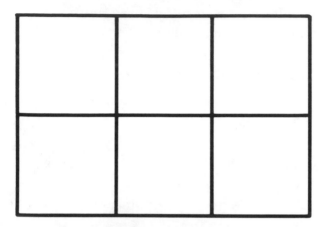

STEP 3: Show $\frac{2}{3}$ on the grid by shading 2 of the 3 columns. Since columns are up-and-down rows, use up-and-down lines to shade them.

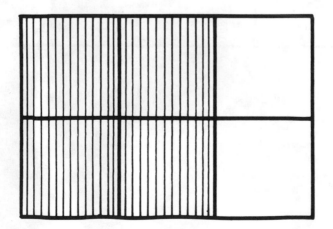

STEP 4: Show $\frac{1}{2}$ on the grid by shading 1 of the 2 left-to-right rows. Use left-to-right lines to shade them.

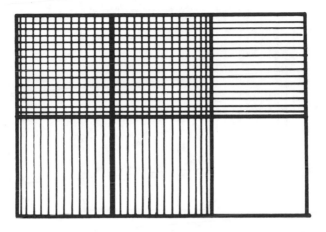

STEP 5: Add up the number of squares shaded both ways. This is the numerator of the answer.

NUMERATOR

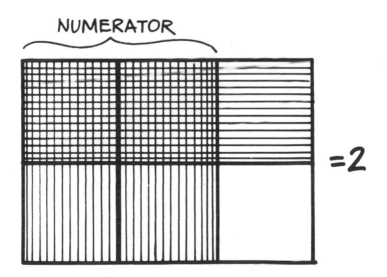

=2

STEP 6: The denominator is the total number of squares.

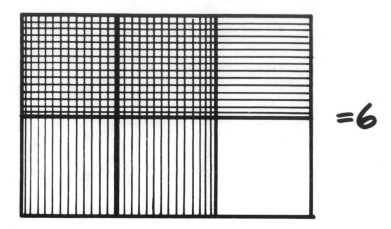

3. Multiply fractions the easy way.

TIP: Remember "Top x Top and Bottom x Bottom."

EXAMPLE

Multiply $\frac{3}{4}$ by $\frac{4}{5}$.

$$\frac{3}{4} \times \frac{4}{5} = \frac{3 \times 4}{4 \times 5} = \frac{12}{20}$$

The answer is $\frac{12}{20}$, or $\frac{3}{5}$.

4. Divide fractions the easy way.

TIP: Remember "Flip the Second Fraction Upside Down."

EXAMPLE

Divide $\frac{3}{4}$ by $\frac{4}{5}$.

FIRST, $\frac{4}{5}$ becomes $\frac{5}{4}$.

NEXT, do "Top x Top and Bottom x Bottom."

$$\frac{3}{4} \text{ x } \frac{5}{4} = \frac{3 \text{ x } 5}{4 \text{ x } 4} = \frac{15}{16}$$

The answer is $\frac{15}{16}$.

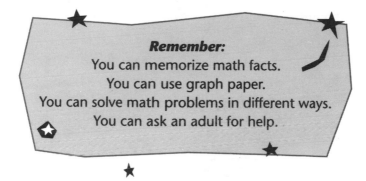

Remember:
You can memorize math facts.
You can use graph paper.
You can solve math problems in different ways.
You can ask an adult for help.

PART THREE:

WAYS TO KEEP SCHOOL COOL

Chapter 13

You Can Get Along With Others

Many students with LD do not like school. Some do not like it because they have trouble with their school work. But most do not like it because they have trouble getting along with others. In fact, they say this is a bigger problem for them than their school work.

Kids can be unkind. Sometimes they tease you or ignore you for no reason. But at other times, they may have a reason. You may have said or done something they did not like. Even if you did not mean for them to get angry, this is what happened.

There seem to be four main reasons why kids with LD have trouble getting along with others. It will help you to know about these and what you can do about them.

Reason #1: Saying Or Doing Things Without Thinking

Kevin is in the same class as Julie. One day Julie comes to school with a new haircut. Kevin says, "Your hair looks really ugly!" He says this in front of the whole class.

Kai goes to sharpen her pencil. She passes Vinny's desk and sees a book she wants to look at. Kai grabs the book without asking Vinny if it is okay. When Vinny complains, Kai has to stay in from recess.

Do you say or do things without thinking? This is called "being impulsive." Here are two things you can do about it.

Impulsive

im PUL siv

1. *Think before you act.*

Everybody has thoughts about saying or doing things that are not okay. But you do not have to act on these thoughts.

Instead, you can STOP. Then ask yourself, "How will that person feel if I say what I'm thinking?" Or, "What will happen to me if I do that?" Or, "How would I like it if someone did that to me?"

Kevin could have told himself, "If I tell Julie her hair looks ugly, it will hurt her feelings." Kai could have told herself, "If I take Vinny's book, I'll get in trouble."

2. Do something else instead.

When you feel like saying something that is not okay, put your hand over your mouth. Turn away from the person, if you can. This will give you time to think before you talk. You can decide if it is a good idea to say what you were thinking.

When you feel like grabbing something, put your hands in your pockets. Keep them there. Think about what will happen if you grab.

Reason #2: Trouble With Talking And Listening

The other kids think Treena is funny. They laugh at the things she says. But Treena does not mean to be funny. She gets mad when the other kids laugh. She swears at them, throws things, and tries to hit them. Treena does not have many friends. She is very unhappy.

Brian is the class clown. Whenever he goes to the blackboard, he tips his desk and chair over and trips. The other students always laugh. They also laugh at the things he says. Brian pretends that he says funny things on purpose, just like when he tips his desk over. But sometimes he feels confused. He does not understand why the things he says are funny.

Do you have trouble saying what you mean? Do people think you are trying to be funny when you are not? Is it hard for you to understand what other people are saying? This is called a "language learning disability." Here are four things you can do about it.

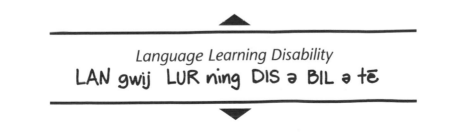

Language Learning Disability
LAN gwij LUR ning DIS ə BIL ə tē

1. Plan what you want to say.

You cannot always plan what you will say before you say it. But you can try. This will help you to not say things you do not mean.

For example: Your teacher has given you an assignment. You will have to discuss a current event in class. You can plan what you will say. Practice in front of the mirror. Practice with your family or friends.

2. Become an expert.

It is easier to talk about something you know a lot about. It is easier to understand other people who like the same things you do.

You can become an expert. (People with LD can become experts, just like anyone else.) You might pick something other kids are interested in. What about baseball cards? Music? Old movies? Comics?

3. Stick up for yourself.

You will learn more about this in Chapter 14. For now, just know this: You can tell someone how you feel without getting angry.

What if another person makes fun of something you said? You can look the person in the eye and say, "I do not like to be made fun of." You may need to say this more than once. The person still may not stop making fun of you. But you will feel better because you stuck up for yourself. And you will not get into trouble.

4. Stay away from people who tease.

Maybe you cannot control your language learning disability. But you can control who you choose to hang around with.

Do you try to be friends with some kids because they are popular? If they make fun of you, they are not good choices for friends. Do you know other kids who do not tease and are kind to others? Maybe they are not the most popular kids. Still, they might be very good choices for friends.

Talk this over with an adult you trust. Find out what the adult thinks about which kids would make better friends for you.

Reason #3: Trouble With Sports Or Games

Jesse hates soccer and kickball. He is always the last person picked to be on a team. The other students make fun of him because he is not very good at sports. He feels left out. He avoids team games at recess so he will not be teased about the way he plays.

Do you have trouble with sports and games that involve throwing, catching, or kicking? This is called a "motor coordination" problem. Here are three things you can do about it.

Motor Coordination

MŌ tər kō ÔR dn Ā shən

1. Choose the game you are best at. Then practice, practice, practice.

Pick one game you really like. Decide that you will get better at it. Then do it!

For example: You like soccer a lot. You want to be a better soccer player. So you take a soccer ball up to the field after school or on the weekend. You practice your kicking. Maybe you ask a brother or sister, parent or friend to roll the ball so you can kick it.

Do not try to become an expert at every game. Just pick one you enjoy and other kids play. Then do your best. Spend time working on your skills. You may not become a great player. But you may become good enough to play without getting teased.

2. Try something else.

There are other kids who do not play team games. Look around and see what they are doing. Maybe they are swinging or climbing on monkey bars. Maybe they are playing games with one or two other people, like hopscotch. See if you can join them.

3. *Start something new.*

Do you have a good idea for a game or activity at recess? Maybe you can organize it. Ask a couple of kids you like if they want to join you. If you need help getting started, ask an adult.

Reason #4: Trouble With Feelings

Sarah is on the playground at recess. She wants to play tetherball with Ricky. She does not know that Ricky is unhappy. He just got yelled at by the playground teacher. He is frowning and hanging his head.

Sarah sees the way Ricky looks. But she does not understand what it means. "Let's play ball!" she shouts.

"Go away," Ricky says. "Leave me alone." Now Sarah's feelings are hurt.

Do you have trouble figuring out how people are feeling? Is it hard for you to see the "signals" people give out to show how they feel? This is called a "social skills deficit" or "social perceptual disability." Here are three things you can do about it.

Social Skills Deficit
SŌ shəl skils DEF ə sit
Social Perceptual Disability
SŌ shəl per SEP chŏŏ əl DIS ə BIL ə tē

1. Ask for help with your social skills.

Talk to your school counselor, psychologist, or social worker. These people know how to help young people with their social skills. If your school does not have a counselor, psychologist, or social worker, talk to your teacher or principal. Explain that you need help learning how to get along with others.

2. Stop, look, and listen.

Before you go up to other people, look at their faces. Are they smiling or frowning? Before you go up to a group, pay attention. Are they talking and laughing? Do they sound angry? Are they quiet? Are they busy doing something? Will you be interrupting if you go up to them?

Try to figure out how people are feeling before you talk to them. If this is very hard for you, ask an adult to point out some of the signals people send. These signals can tell you how other people are feeling.

3. Listen carefully. Ask questions.

Everybody likes to have somebody listen to them. When another person is talking to you, do not think about what you want to say. Instead, listen very carefully to what the other person is saying. Then ask questions to show that you were listening.

For example: Your friend says, "That show on TV last night was really cool." You can say, "You really liked it, huh? What was the best part?" This shows that you were listening. It shows that you are interested in what your friend has to say.

Listening and asking questions takes practice. Try it with your family and friends.

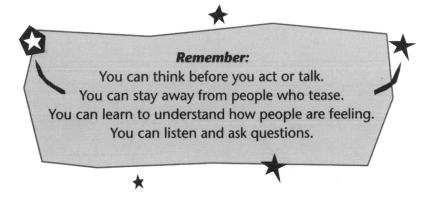

Remember:
You can think before you act or talk.
You can stay away from people who tease.
You can learn to understand how people are feeling.
You can listen and ask questions.

Chapter 14
You Can Stick Up For Yourself

It feels great when someone helps you out or takes your side in an argument. It feels really good when someone tries to change things to make your life easier. Maybe teachers, parents, and friends have done things like this for you. For example, maybe a teacher stepped in when a much bigger kid was pushing you around.

But what if other people always have to help you or defend you? What if you always need someone else to make sure things go your way? You may never learn to take care of yourself. You may never learn to stick up for yourself.

There are different ways to stick up for yourself. Some of these are not very helpful. Some are very helpful.

Not Very Helpful Ways To Stick Up For Yourself

Being passive

Someone has taken money from Reggie's desk. Reggie tells Nancy, "I think Tom took it." When Nancy tells Tom, Tom says, "You tell Reggie I didn't take his money."

This is not very helpful. Tom does not know what Nancy will say to Reggie. Maybe she will say, "Well, Tom says he didn't take it, but I don't believe him." Tom needs to speak for himself.

Passive people are not direct in what they say and do. They may talk to someone else instead of the person they really should talk to. They may mumble or talk in a very soft voice. They may look at the floor instead of at the person they are talking to. Not many people listen to them or believe them.

Being aggressive

Aggressive

ə GRES iv

Arnold looked at his math assignment. The problems were too hard! He could never get them right! He cried and screamed. He was so upset that his teacher let him skip the assignment.

After that, whenever Arnold did not want to do his work, he cried and screamed. Soon none of the other kids wanted to be his friend. The teacher did not enjoy having him in class. She began to punish him when he cried and screamed.

Aggressive people are too direct in what they say and do. They try to get what they want with a loud, angry voice, or with force. This may work at first, but it does not work for long. People do not like to be pushed around. And there is always someone else who is louder, angrier, or stronger.

Helpful Ways
To Stick Up For Yourself

Be assertive

Assertive
ə SUR tiv

You can be direct without being loud or angry. You can help yourself without being selfish. You can say what you think and still listen to other people.

Nobody gets what they want all the time. But you are more likely to get what you want if you are assertive. Even if you do not get what you want, you will still feel good about yourself. You will know that you did your best.

Here is how to be assertive.

★ Talk in a medium tone of voice, not too loud and not too soft.

★ Look the other person in the eye. Do not look at your shoes or the sky.

★ Make suggestions. Do not make demands.

★ If you do not get what you want, thank the person for listening. Try again another time. Do not make threats.

Being assertive is a skill. It takes practice. It can be scary, because you do not know how other people will react. If you have never been assertive around adults, they will be surprised. They may keep treating you in the same old ways. You will just have to keep being assertive. They will get used to the new you.

Practice being assertive

There is a safe way to practice being assertive. Ask an adult to help you "role-play" different scenes.

When you role-play, you act out what other people might say or do. Ask your classroom teacher, your LD teacher, a parent, or another adult to help you. Or you can ask your school counselor, psychologist, or social worker. It is best to do role plays with someone who can give you ideas about being assertive.

Here are some scenes you can role-play. Or make up scenes from your own life.

★ You have trouble with reading. It is especially hard for you to read out loud, in front of other people. It makes you feel embarrassed. But your classroom teacher keeps asking you to read in front of the class. He says you need the practice. What can you do?

    Idea: You can talk to your teacher in private. You can say, "I know I need practice with reading. But it is hard for me to read out loud in front of the whole class. I get really embarrassed. I could read out loud, just to you, after class. Would that be okay?"

★ Your history teacher gives a test every week. It is always a 30-minute test. You know the material, but you write very slowly. You can never finish the test on time. What can you do?

    Idea: You can talk to your teacher in private. You can say, "I know the material. I don't finish on time because I write too slowly. Can I take the next test on a tape recorder? I can say my answers into the tape recorder. Then you will see that I know the material. Can we try it?"

★ You do okay in math, but the other kids know you have LD. One day, your math teacher divides your class into "teams." Some of the kids on your team complain. They say that you will lower the team's score.

Idea: You can say, "I know you think I will hurt the team's score. But give me a chance. I do pretty well in math." If the kids will not listen, do not get angry. Do not get back at them by trying to hurt the team's score. Just do your best and work hard. Let your work speak for itself.

Remember:
You can learn to stick up for yourself.
You can talk in a medium tone of voice, look the other person in the eye, and make suggestions.
You can practice being assertive.

Chapter 15

You Can Handle Conflict With Others

School is tough enough without arguments and fights. All kids have troubles at school, but some kids with LD seem to have more troubles than other students. Maybe it is because they are frustrated with their school work. They get angry and blow up too fast. Or maybe it is because they do not know how to handle conflict with others.

There are ways to make your school work easier. You are learning some of them in this book. There are also ways to handle conflict so everybody wins. You can learn these, too.

Seven Steps To A Solution

Imagine that you have a friend named Alex. You and Alex are on a baseball team together. You enjoy playing at recess, except that Alex always argues about the rules. These arguments interrupt your games. Sometimes everybody gets mad and quits.

What can you do? You can ignore the problem until your team breaks up. You can ask an adult to solve your problem for you. Or you can follow these seven steps and solve it yourself.

TIP: While you are following these steps, remember to be assertive. You learned about this in Chapter 14 on pages 120–122. You may want to go back and read those pages again.

Step 1: Tell the other person how you see the problem.

There is a special way to do this. It is called an "I-message." An I-message goes like this.

"I feel..."   Use a word or words to describe how you feel. You might say "sad," "upset," "angry," or "hurt."

"...when you..."   Describe what the other person is doing to cause the conflict or keep it going.

"...because..."   Tell how the conflict is affecting you.

You might tell Alex, "I feel upset when you argue about the rules all the time because we don't get to play and everybody gets mad."

Step 2: Listen to what the other person has to say about the problem.

Listen even if you do not like what the other person is saying. Listen even if you think the other person is wrong. Listen very carefully, and do not interrupt. You will need this information for Step 3.

Step 3: Repeat what the other person thinks the problem is. Repeat what you think the problem is. Then ask, "What should we do?"

You might say, "Okay. You think people are cheating when we play baseball. I think your arguing slows the game down and sometimes makes it stop. What should we do?"

Step 4: Brainstorm ways to solve the problem.

There are three simple rules for brainstorming.

 First, everybody tries to come up with as many ideas as they can. These can be serious, silly, or in-between.

 Second, all ideas are okay during brainstorming.

 Third, nobody makes fun of anybody else's ideas. Nobody puts anyone down.

You and Alex might brainstorm these ideas:

(a) stop playing baseball

(b) do not let Alex play

(c) stop cheating

(d) choose someone in the game to settle all arguments

(e) agree on rules before starting a game

(f) go get a teacher when there is an argument

Step 5: Decide on a solution.

Look at the list of brainstormed ideas. Work together to decide on the best one. You both have to agree on which one to try.

For example: You do not want to stop playing. Alex wants to keep playing. So ideas (a) and (b) will not work.

Alex is the one who thinks people are cheating. This is not the way you see the problem. So idea (c) will not work.

Everybody agrees on the rules before starting to play. The arguments are about what happens after the games start. So idea (e) will not work.

Getting a teacher seems like a good idea. But it might take too long. Waiting for a teacher will interrupt your games. So idea (f) will not work.

Idea (d) is looking pretty good. Maybe you could elect an "umpire" before each game. Everyone could agree to let the umpire settle all arguments.

You and Alex decide that idea (d) is the one to try.

Step 6: Decide how to do it.

You and Alex agree to take this idea to the rest of the players. Everybody talks over how to do it.

You all decide that the umpire should be on a different team each game. Since nobody wants to sit out for a game, the umpire will get to play. The players on one team will elect an umpire from the other team. That way, they can elect the person they think will be the most fair.

Step 7: Decide if it works.

You need a way to "evaluate" your solution. To evaluate it means to study it, think about it, and decide if it works.

Evaluate
i VAL yo͞o ĀT

Your team tries the umpire idea for three games. Then the players talk about it. Everybody agrees that the umpire helps cut down on arguments and delays. Now you know that your solution works.

Practice Solving Problems

In following the seven steps, be sure to keep your cool. If you get mad or aggressive, the steps will not work. If the other person gets mad, do not back down or become passive. Try again another time.

Practice these steps until you get used to them. Ask someone to role-play them with you. This can be a brother or sister or friend. It can be a teacher or parent. When you feel okay with the steps, try them out on a real problem you are having with a friend.

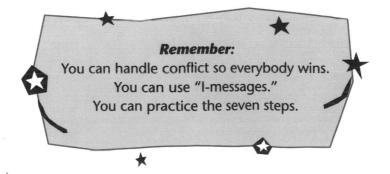

Remember:
You can handle conflict so everybody wins.
You can use "I-messages."
You can practice the seven steps.

Chapter 16

Eight Ways To Rescue Recess

Terese thinks recess is great. She likes it because it is a break from school work. She has fun with her friends.

Ethan hates recess. He always gets teased. He never has anyone to play with.

Who are you most like, Terese or Ethan? If you want to make recess better, try some of the ideas in this chapter.

1. Find Someone To Play With

If you are alone, look around for someone else who is alone, too. Choose a game and ask that person to play with you.

2. Join Games

Look for games where kids line up to play and take turns. Get in line to play.

3. Start Early

Try to get involved in a game at the beginning of recess. It may be harder to join later, when the game is already started.

4. Bring Something Fun From Home

If your school allows this, bring something fun from home to play with at recess. Ask someone to play with you.

5. Pick The Right People To Play With

Watch the other students on the playground. See who plays without teasing or fighting. Pick these people to play with.

6. Stay Away From Troublemakers

There are kids who always seem to be in trouble at recess. You know who they are. Stay away from them! They may let you play with them, but you could get in trouble, too.

7. Stay Out Of Trouble

Do not do things at recess which could get you in trouble. Do not climb a fence you are not supposed to climb. Do not grab a ball from other kids. You may get attention for doing these things, but it is not worth it.

If you say or do things without thinking, you may have a problem with being impulsive. You learned about this in Chapter 13 on pages 107–109. You may want to go back and read those pages again.

8. Get Help If You Need It

If you try these ideas and you still have trouble with recess, get help. Ask a teacher or school counselor to watch what happens on the playground. Explain how you feel about recess. Tell your helper that you need more ideas for making recess better.

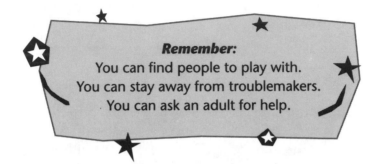

Remember:
You can find people to play with.
You can stay away from troublemakers.
You can ask an adult for help.

Chapter 17

You Can Stay Out Of Trouble

School is not cool when you are in trouble all the time. Some students with LD get into trouble a lot. Some have problems with being impulsive. Others get frustrated with their school work and start acting up. Others get into trouble as a way to get attention.

You already know some ways to stay out of trouble. In Chapter 13, you learned how to think before you act. In Chapter 14, you learned how to stick up for yourself. You can use these skills in many ways.

For example: Jerome liked a girl in his class named Melanie. He wanted to talk to her at recess. So he passed her a note, asking her to wait for him by the door. But the teacher caught Jerome passing the note. He had to stay inside for recess.

Jerome did not think before he acted. He could have asked himself, "Will I get in trouble if I get caught passing a note?" The answer would have been "yes." He could have asked himself, "Will it be worth it?" The answer would have been "no." By getting caught, he lost his chance to talk to Melanie at recess.

David's story is different. When his friend, Mark, asked him to skip school with him, David stuck up for himself. He looked Mark in the eye and said, "No. If we skip school, we could get in trouble. Besides, I want to play tetherball at recess. How about it?"

Because staying out of trouble is so important, here are even more ways you can manage it.

Learn The School Rules

Lots of kids get into trouble because they do not know the school rules. Do you know the rules in your school? Do you know the rules in your classroom? If you do not, or if you are not sure, ask your teacher what the rules are. If you think you cannot remember them, ask your teacher to write them down for you. Also ask the teacher what happens when you break the rules.

Take the rules home and learn them. If there are any you do not understand, ask your parents or an older brother or sister to explain them to you.

Avoid People, Places, And Things Where Trouble Is Likely

You might know some kids who like to do things that cause trouble. Avoid hanging around them. You might know some places in school where trouble often happens. Maybe there is a certain bathroom or a part of the playground. Stay away from those places. If some school equipment is off limits without a teacher present, obey these rules.

When The Routine Changes, Keep Your Cool

Kids often get into trouble when the school routine changes. One of the biggest problem times is when there is a substitute teacher.

Substitute

SUB sti TOOT

A substitute may not know about your LD, and may not act the same way your regular teacher does. You may feel frustrated by the assignments you are given. Also, a substitute may not know how your class works. Other students may take advantage of this. You may want to join in and do things you are not supposed to do.

Think before you act! Be especially careful to follow school rules on days like this. If you feel frustrated, tell the substitute. Raise your hand during a quiet time and explain your LD. For example, you might say, "I have trouble with writing. I usually read my answers into a tape recorder. The tape recorder is in the closet. Can I get it?"

Or you could ask your regular teacher to leave a note for the substitute. The note could tell about your LD.

Holidays can be problem times, too. Days right before holidays or vacations are full of excitement and changes in the school routine. Some kids are bothered by these changes and get into trouble.

On special days, tell yourself in the morning to keep your cool. Maybe you and your teacher can work out a quiet, secret signal. Your teacher can use the signal to let you know if you start to act up.

What To Do If You Get Into Serious Trouble

We know how hard school can be for kids with LD. You try your best, but sometimes you fail anyway. You feel lonely, but you may not know how to make and keep friends. You want your teachers to like you, but you cannot seem to please them.

Some kids with LD get frustrated. And some get mad.

Felipe's Story

When Felipe was in the sixth grade, there was a student in his class who teased him all the time. The student's name was Brad. "Why can't you read?" Brad would say. "You must really be stupid." Or, "What a retard. The retard can't read!"

One day at recess, Brad called Felipe some bad names. He yelled them out in front of everybody. Felipe lost control of himself. He turned around and threw Brad down on the ground as hard as he could. Brad hit his head on a rock and did not get up.

Felipe was afraid and ran to get his teacher. When the teacher saw Brad, she ran to the office to call an ambulance. The ambulance came and took Brad to the hospital. Brad had a concussion—a bruised brain. He had to stay in the hospital for several days.

The teacher and principal did not know why Felipe threw Brad on the ground. They just knew that Brad had been hurt. They suspended Felipe from school for a week. Felipe was in serious trouble. On top of that, he felt terrible about hurting Brad.

Cynthia's Story

Cynthia was sad because she did not have any friends. It seemed that nobody in the whole eighth grade wanted to be her friend.

One day a group of girls told Cynthia that they would be her friends if she did something for them. Cynthia felt happy. She would finally have friends! "What do you want me to do?" she asked the girls.

"Get your teacher's keys to the school building," they said. "Then give them to us."

Later that day, just before recess, Cynthia told her teacher she did not feel well. Her teacher trusted Cynthia. She gave Cynthia permission to stay in the room during recess, all by herself.

As soon as everyone was gone, Cynthia opened her teacher's desk drawer. Sure enough, the keys were there. Before recess was over, Cynthia met one of her "new friends" in the bathroom. She gave her the keys to the building. At the end of school, Cynthia rushed out of the building before her teacher could notice the missing keys.

When Cynthia came to school the next day, the police were there. Somebody had broken into the school during the night. They had destroyed many of the papers in the principal's office. They had wrecked many of the classrooms.

Cynthia's teacher suspected that Cynthia had stolen her keys. She reported this to the principal. Cynthia was called to the principal's office. She told the principal and her teacher that she had taken the keys to give to her friends. Cynthia was suspended from school for the rest of the year.

We hope that you never get into serious trouble. But if you do, you can still help yourself. Here are three things you can do for yourself.

1. Talk to an adult you trust.

When Felipe hurt Brad, his teacher and principal did not know why. They did not know that Brad teased Felipe all the time. Felipe could have told his teacher about the teasing. This would not have made Brad's hurt go away. But it might have helped the teacher to understand Felipe better.

If you get into serious trouble, talk to an adult you trust. Try to explain what happened. Tell how you got into trouble. Be honest about what you did. Do not cover up for anybody else. Make sure that everyone knows how sorry you are.

See if the adult will talk to the principal for you. Maybe the adult can make the principal understand.

In Chapter 8, you learned how to get help from adults. You may want to go back and read that chapter again.

2. Learn a lesson from the experience.

No matter how mad you feel, no matter how much you want friends, this is not worth getting into serious trouble. Talk to an adult you trust. Tell the adult about your feelings and your frustration. Ask for ideas—what can you do about your feelings?

Do not hurt another person. Do not let someone else talk you into doing something wrong. *Anyone who tries to get you to do something wrong is not your friend.* This is the lesson Cynthia learned from her experience.

3. Do not give up.

Both Felipe and Cynthia were suspended from school. Both went back to school when the suspension was over. At first, they felt afraid. They felt embarrassed. They knew that people would make fun of them. But they went back anyway.

Some students who get suspended give up on school. They never go back again. They are making a big mistake.

It is true that school may be harder for you than it is for other kids. It may seem that no one at school likes you or cares about you. Especially if you get into serious trouble, you may want to give up on school.

Do not give up! Instead, find an adult you can talk to. There is sure to be one adult at school you can trust. There is sure to be one who will listen to you. Go to that person when you feel like giving up.

Do not let selfish, uncaring people be the reason for you to quit school. If you do, you will be giving them power over you. You will be letting them control a big part of your life. Kids who drop out of school have a tough time finding a good job.

Do not drop out! Instead, stay out of trouble in the future. You can succeed. And you can be a stronger person than many other people who do not have LD.

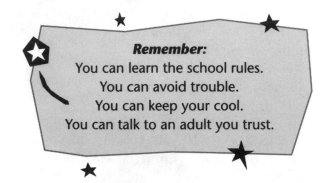

Remember:
You can learn the school rules.
You can avoid trouble.
You can keep your cool.
You can talk to an adult you trust.

Chapter 18
You Can Succeed!

We named this book *The School Survival Guide* because we know that school can be hard for kids with LD. But we also know that you can succeed.

You can succeed while you are still in school. You can succeed after you leave school. And you can succeed in life.

How can we be sure? Because we know people like Alejandra, Jonathon, and William. They have LD, and they are succeeding. Read their stories and see for yourself.

Alejandra's Story

We met Alejandra when she was 12 years old. She worked hard in school. She was never shy about asking her teachers for help. She worked so hard that she did not have much time left for friends and fun.

Alejandra had a dream. Her dream was to get a college degree someday.

Alejandra understood that she could not get a college degree just by wanting one. She knew she would have to take steps to make her dream come true.

Alejandra set goals for herself. First, she would graduate from high school with a B average. Next, she would get into a college. Then she would graduate from college.

Her goals did not stop there. She decided what she would do after college. She would become a teacher of other kids with LD.

It took a long time, but Alejandra reached her goals. They did not all turn out exactly the way she planned. But they were good enough.

She graduated from high school with a C-plus average. This was not the B average she had wanted. But she did not give up. She kept working toward her goals.

She got into a college. Most students graduate from college in four years. It took Alejandra six years. But this did not bother her. She found that the longer she stayed in school, the more she learned. She graduated from college with a B average.

When Alejandra graduated from college, she looked for a job. She wanted to be a teacher of kids with LD. She got a job as a resource room teacher for third-grade and fourth-grade kids with LD.

Today Alejandra has been a teacher for three years. She loves her job. She loves the kids in her class. Most of all, she loves helping kids with LD plan for their own futures.

Jonathon's Story

Jonathon is in the eighth grade. He has a hard time with reading and math. He does not do well in these classes. But there are other things he does very well.

Jonathon is an artist. He makes beautiful prints through a process called "silk screen." Many of his prints hang in the school hallway. Sometimes he even takes his prints to art shows. He has sold many of his prints.

Jonathon plans to be an artist full-time when he graduates from high school. He may go to an art school, or he may try to find a job with a printing company. He has not made up his mind which one he will do.

Jonathon does not feel bad because he gets poor grades in reading and math. He knows that many kids who get good grades do not have his talent. Jonathon feels good about himself because of his talent.

William's Story

William is 26 years old. He had a hard time while he was in school. But William is a good worker.

Ever since he was 12 years old, William has had jobs. He knows how important it is to get to work on time. He knows that he should call his boss if he is sick and cannot go to work.

Today William is a clerk at a supermarket. He loves his job. He enjoys seeing his favorite customers. William's boss wishes that he had ten workers just like William.

William did not graduate from college. He is not an artist. But he is a success. He has his own car. He lives in his own apartment. Most important, he feels good about himself. He is proud of himself because he is such a good worker.

As you can see, there are many ways to succeed. You can do it, too. Just think about what you want to be someday. Set goals for yourself. Start taking steps to reach your goals.

If you work hard, if you do not give up, you will reach your goals. Like Alejandra, Jonathon, and William, you will succeed.

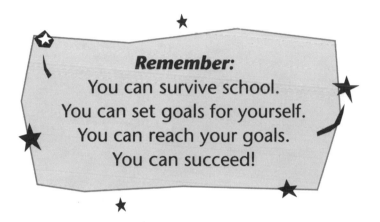

Remember:
You can survive school.
You can set goals for yourself.
You can reach your goals.
You can succeed!

RESOURCES

MY ROUTINE

TIME	MON	TUES	WED	THURS	FRI
__:__					
__:__					
__:__					
__:__					
__:__					
__:__					
__:__					
__:__					
__:__					
__:__					
__:__					
__:__					
__:__					
__:__					
__:__					
__:__					

TIME CHART

Day: _____

Activity   **Time**

_____   _____

_____   _____

_____   _____

_____   _____

_____   _____

_____   _____

_____   _____

_____   _____

_____   _____

_____   _____

_____   _____

_____   _____

_____   _____

_____   _____

_____   _____

_____   _____

THINGS TO DO

Day: _____

**Check off   Activity
when done**

_____   _____

_____   _____

_____   _____

_____   _____

_____   _____

_____   _____

_____   _____

_____   _____

_____   _____

_____   _____

_____   _____

_____   _____

_____   _____

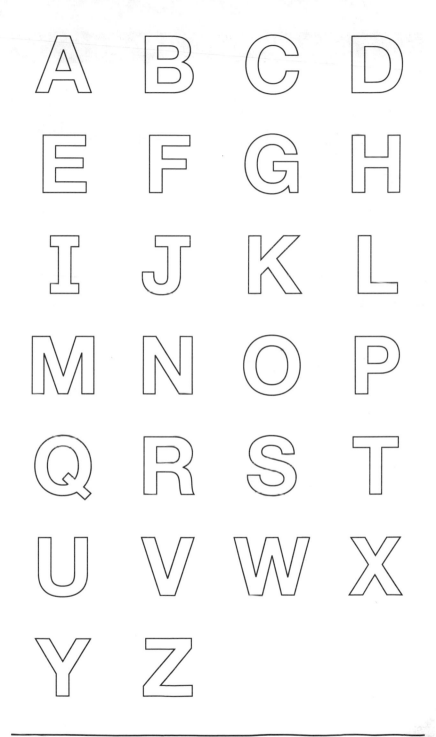

CROSSWORD PUZZLE FORM

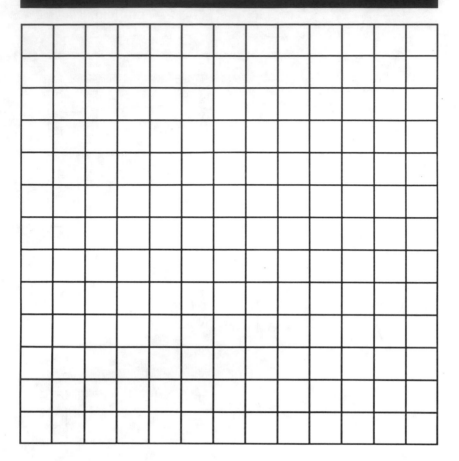

References

Chapter 7

Bley, N. S., and C. A. Thornton, *Teaching Mathematics to the Learning Disabled* (Austin, TX: Pro-Ed, 1989).

Bos, C., and S. Vaughn, *Strategies for Teaching Students with Learning and Behavior Problems* (Boston: Allyn and Bacon, Inc., 1988).

Chapter 9

Lerner, J. W., *Learning Disabilities: Theories, Diagnosis, and Teaching Strategies*, 5th ed. (Boston: Houghton Mifflin Co., 1988).

Mercer, C. D., and A. R. Mercer, *Teaching Students with Learning Problems* (Columbus, OH: Charles E. Merrill, 1981).

Chapter 10

Lerner, J. W., *Learning Disabilities: Theories, Diagnosis, and Teaching Strategies*, 5th ed. (Boston: Houghton Mifflin Co., 1988).

Mercer, C. D., and A. R. Mercer, *Teaching Students with Learning Problems* (Columbus, OH: Charles E. Merrill, 1981).

Polloway, E. A., J. R. Patton, J. S. Payne, and R. A. Payne, *Strategies for Teaching Learners with Special Needs*, 4th ed. (Columbus, OH: Charles E. Merrill, 1989).

Chapter 11

Krevisky, J., and J. Linfield, *The Bad Speller's Dictionary* (New York: Random House, 1963).

Wittels, H., and Greisman, Joan, *A Dictionary of Commonly Mispelled Words* (New York: Grosset & Dunlap, 1973).

Chapter 12

Bley, N. S., and C. A. Thornton, *Teaching Mathematics to the Learning Disabled* (Austin, TX: Pro-Ed, 1989).

Hutchings, B., *Low-Stress Algorithms* (Reston, VA.: National Council of Teachers of Mathematics, 1976).

Lerner, J. W., *Learning Disabilities: Theories, Diagnosis, and Teaching Strategies*, 5th ed. (Boston: Houghton Mifflin Co., 1988).

Mercer, C. D., and A. R. Mercer, *Teaching Students with Learning Problems* (Columbus, OH: Charles E. Merrill, 1981).

Ruais, R. W. "A Low-Stress Algorithm for Fractions," *Mathematics Teacher*, 71, 258-260, 1978.

154

Recommended Learning and Teaching Materials

Ordering Information
The materials recommended in this section are available from the following publishers. Addresses and telephone numbers are listed here for your convenience. Call or write to request catalogs and additional information.

Academic Therapy Publications
High Noon Books
20 Commercial Boulevard
Novato, CA 94949-6191
(415) 883-3314

American Guidance Service (AGS)
4201 Woodland Road
P.O. Box 99
Circle Pines, MN 55014-1796
(800) 328-2560

Childswork Childsplay
Center for Applied Psychology
441 N. 5th Street, Third Floor
Philadelphia, PA 19123
(215) 592-1141

Free Spirit Publishing Inc.
400 First Avenue North, Suite 616
Minneapolis, MN 55401-1730
(800) 735-7323

Grosset & Dunlap
Putnam Publishing Group
200 Madison Avenue
New York, NY 10016
(800) 631-8571

New American Library (Penguin U.S.A.)
375 Hudson Street
New York, NY 10014
(212) 366-2000

Random House
201 E. 50th Street
New York, NY 10022
(800) 726-0600

Research Press
Box 3177
Champaign, IL 61826
(217) 352-3273

SRA/McGraw-Hill (SRA)
P.O. Box 543
Blacklick, OH 43004-0543
(800) 843-8855

Organizational Skills

Crary, Elizabeth, *Pick Up Your Socks and Other Skills Growing Children Need*. A workbook to help parents help children learn about responsibility. (Childswork Childsplay)

Lakein, A., *How to Get Control of Your Time and Your Life*. (New American Library)

Levine, Fredric, and Kathleen Aneasko, *Winning the Homework War*. The authors claim a 90 percent success rate in improving children's study skills. For children ages 6–12. (Childswork Childsplay)

McGinnis, Ellen, and Arnold Goldstein, *Skill-Streaming the Elementary School Child*. (Research Press)

Radencich, Marguerite C., and Jeanne Shay Schumm, *How to Help Your Child with Homework*. Tried-and-true ways to help your child do better in school. (Free Spirit Publishing Inc.)

"HomeWork Coach" offers study-skills strategies for secondary-level students. The kit includes a 58-minute video, a teacher's game plan, and a player's guide for students. (AGS)

School Skills

Reading

"High Hat Early Reading Program" is for remedial reading students, children with learning disabilities, and ESL students. Children move easily from spoken language to written language with songs, games, and stories introduced by High Hat, a "lovable puppet character." (AGS)

"Listen, Speak, Read, and Spell" is a program for grades 3–12 that focuses on basic phonetic skills which are reinforced through auditory and visual methods. The kit includes 11 audio cassettes, 56 spirit masters, card index, 50 award certificates, and a teacher's guide. (SRA)

Many high-interest reading and learning materials are available from High Noon Books, a division of Academic Therapy Publications.

Writing

Dahlstrom, Lorraine, *Doing the Days: A Year's Worth of Creative Journaling, Drawing, Listening, Reading, Thinking, Arts & Crafts Activities for Children Ages 8–12.* 366 writing activities plus over 1,000 more ideas to try. (Free Spirit Publishing Inc.)

Huelsberg, Enid, *Alphabet Mastery* books. These are designed to assist young children with their handwriting. Instruction is offered in both manuscript and cursive. (Academic Therapy Publications)

"Strategies for Effective Writing" by Arnold Cheyney and Charles Mangrum II is a series of five sets that help students recall and master writing techniques such as comparison and contrast, narration, description, persuasion, and exposition. For grades 5–8. (SRA)

"Think and Write" is a set of five kits that provide step-by-step instruction in generating ideas and writing sentences, paragraphs, and compositions. It is designed for elementary and middle school students who have learning differences. (SRA)

Spelling

Krevisky, J., and J. Linfield, *The Bad Speller's Dictionary.* Arranges words alphabetically according to their common misspellings. This great little book can usually be found in any bookstore. (Random House)

Wittels, Harriet, and Joan Greisman, *How To Spell It: A Handbook of Commonly Misspelled Words.* Another "bad speller's dictionary," but we prefer its more positive title, especially for children with learning differences. (Grosset & Dunlap)

"Teaching Resources Spelling Series" emphasizes mastery of crucial spelling rules, phonetic patterns, and frequently misspelled sight words. The series consists of 30 lessons designed for grades 2–7. (SRA)

158

Math, Fractions, and Time

"Getting Started with Story Problems," "How to Solve Story Problems," and "Moving Up in Story Problems" can be started in grade 2 and used up to grade 7 or higher. Children learn how to approach story problems logically. (SRA)

"Ice Cream Cones: Beginning Math Game" provides practice in number recognition and mastery of addition and subtraction facts from sums through 12. (SRA)

KeyMath Activity Pacs are for remedial math students and students with special needs. These provide colorful manipulatives and concrete learning activities. (AGS)

"KeyMath Teach and Practice (TAP)" is suggested for remedial math students and students with special needs. Provides assessment tools and strategies for understanding basic skills. (AGS)

"Mental Math and Estimation" teaches students how to improve mental math and estimating skills. Includes a teacher's guide with teaching suggestions and 128 blackline masters. (SRA)

"Moving Up in Fractions" teaches students to name, compare, add, subtract, multiply, and divide with fractions and mixed numerals. (SRA)

"Moving Up in Numbers" provides valuable reinforcement of essential math skills. Order the intermediate or the advanced set. (SRA)

"Teambuilders: Multiplication" uses baseball and hockey game cards for practice of multiplication facts. (SRA)

SRA offers several games and activities that teach children about time, including laminated teaching clocks and clock puzzles. (SRA)

Social Skills and Self-Esteem

Cain, Barbara S., *Double-Dip Feelings*. Helps elementary-age children understand their emotions. (Childswork Childsplay)

Drew, Naomi, *Learning the Skills of Peacemaking*. An activity guide for elementary-age children on communicating, cooperating, and resolving conflict. (Free Spirit Publishing Inc.)

"Children of Divorce" is a group discussion and skill-building program that helps children deal with feelings about divorce. For grades 3–6. (AGS)

"DUSO-Revised: Developing Understanding of Self and Others" stars Duso the Dolphin, who helps children build self-esteem, social awareness, and problem-solving abilities. For grades K–4. (AGS)

"My Friends and Me" promotes development of personal identity and social skills through stories, activities, and songs. For ages 4–5. (AGS)

"Stress Strategies" is a game designed to help kids overcome stress. Relaxation cards teach simple stress reduction techniques designed for children. For ages 7–12. (Childswork Childsplay)

"Taking Part: Introducing Social Skills to Young Children" teaches young children to make conversation, express themselves, cooperate with others, deal with aggression, and more. For preschool through grade 3. (AGS)

Index

"Strategies for Effective Writing,"
    158
"Stress Strategies," 160
Study methods, 13, 16-18
Success stories, 141-145
*Survival Guide For Kids With LD,
    The*, 34

T

"Taking Part: Introducing Social
    Skills to Young Children," 160
Tape recorders
    use in learning, 19-20
Teachers
    getting help from, 17, 28, 35, 51
    substitute, 135
"Teaching Resources Spelling
    Series," 158
"Teambuilders: Multiplication,"
    159
Teasing
    how to handle, 32, 34-35, 111
Testing
    kinds of, 38-40
    ways to handle, 40-42
"Think and Write," 158
Time
    ways to manage, 7-13
        clock game, 46-47
        estimating, 12, 44, 48
        making lists, 9, 12-13, 44
        using a calendar, 44
        using an assignment book, 10
        using different clocks, 45-46
Time charts, 11, 149
Trouble
    how to avoid, 130-131, 133-140
Typing
    use in learning, 22, 25

W

Winning the Homework War, 157
Word banks, 62-63, 78
Word search puzzle, 80-81
Writing
    ways to improve, 67-75
        connecting the dots, 73
        holding a pencil, 70-71
        keeping paper straight, 69
        posture, 68
        practicing, 67-68, 72, 75
        tracing, 71
        using lined paper, 73-74
        using stencils, 71

Notes

More Free Spirit Books

The Survival Guide for Kids with LD* *(Learning Differences)
by Gary Fisher, Ph.D. and Rhoda Cummings, Ed.D.
Solid information and sound advice for children labeled "learning disabled."
Explains LD in terms kids can understand, defines different kinds of LD,
discusses LD programs, and emphasizes that kids with LD can be winners, too.
Ages 8–12; reading level 2.7 (grade 2, 7th month).
$9.95; 104 pp.; illust.; s/c; 6" x 9"

Also available:
The Survival Guide for Kids with LD Audio Cassette
96 minutes on 1 cassette
Cassette only: $10.00
Book with cassette: $16.95

Understanding LD* *(Learning Differences):
A Curriculum to Promote LD Awareness, Self-Esteem,
and Coping Skills in Students Ages 8–13
by Susan McMurchie
Based on Free Spirit's *Survival Guide for Kids with LD* and *School Survival Guide for Kids with LD*, this comprehensive curriculum of 23 lessons helps students with LD become more aware of their learning differences and more positive about their capabilities. Includes dozens of reproducible handouts.
$21.95; 160 pp.; s/c; 8 1/2" x 11"

The Survival Guide for Teenagers with LD*
*(Learning Differences)
by Rhoda Cummings, Ed.D., and Gary Fisher, Ph.D.
Advice, information, and resources to help teenagers with LD succeed at school
and prepare for life as adults. Topics include LD programs, legal rights and
responsibilities related to LD, jobs, dating, and making friends. Ages 13 and up.
$11.95; 200 pp.; illust.; s/c; 6" x 9"

Also available:
The Survival Guide for Teenagers with LD Audio Cassettes
226 minutes on 2 cassettes
Cassettes only: $19.95
Book with cassettes: $28.90

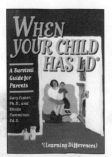

When Your Child Has LD* *(Learning Differences):
A Survival Guide for Parents
by Gary Fisher, Ph.D., and Rhoda Cummings, Ed.D.
This guide gives parents the information and support they need to meet the
challenge of raising a child with learning differences. Written in clear,
understandable language, it empowers parents to advocate for their children
and also to take care of themselves. For parents of children ages 5 and up.
$12.95; 168 pp.; illust.; s/c; 6" x 9"